T0405540

the quality of light in alabama

—jerry hoffman

The only intellectually honest stance
is ambivalence. Or not.

jh

Library of Congress Control Number: 2007903803
ISBN: Hardcover 978-1-4257-6198-1
Softcover 978-1-4257-6196-7

This book was printed in the United States of America.

To order additional copies of this book, contact:
Xlibris Corporation
1-888-795-4274
www.Xlibris.com
Orders@Xlibris.com

40473

CONTENTS

To two generations of my law students at the University of Alabama School of Law and to the poet in all of us.

acknowledgments

Loving thanks to my lifemate, Carol L. Hoffman, generally for hanging in there with me and especially for her creativity and interest in helping me with this book's cover designs, including her givingness in permitting me the use of two of her common-law copyrighted photographs. The photograph integrated into the front cover design she took on one of our pilgrimages to Cheaha State Park, Alabama. The photograph appearing on the back cover she took of me blocking out a few of the many beautiful flowers and flower gardens at Bellingrath Gardens, Alabama. She and her photographs have recorded and enhanced the quality of light in Alabama.

And I won't soon forget Ms. Tiffany Arranguez and her staff at Xlibris for their participation in the cover designs and for her patience and care in watching over the production of this book.

jh

City Café

"Entering City Café in Northport's historic downtown
feels like stepping into a time capsule. This Alabama
place hails from a simpler time . . . ."
http://datelinealabama.com/article/2002/10/08

The Past is not a place.
You can't go there for breakfast; greet the waitress of familiar face
who brings the usual; nurse a mug of coffee pressed between your palms,
as if praying alms
of Time;
through the store-front window watch the red sun climb
a many-sherbet lattice-work of cloud;
behind you hear a sudden laugh out loud
rise above the pooled voice of old men
gathered Once Again
(even though
there is no Once Before, despite the seeming so)
gathered once again to celebrate the moment in the name of moments
somehow
like those framed remembrances of Now
hanging in untutored ranks and files on the paneled wall
behind the counter, of Nows they knew, these ghosts, and Nows they never
knew at all;
lean back in the high-backed booth
and, doing so, lean backward into youth,
or even into the breath just now gone by;
in the corner of your eye,
apprehend those others hunched on counter stools,
working men in working clothes lingering from Now to Now as their
coffee cools;
stand at the cashbox, smiling; joshing, pay
two-fifty-six including tax; step back into the street, into Today.
Today is not to save, nor yet to borrow.
Yesterday is not a time, nor is Tomorrow.

Sonnet No. 4

Don't say to me, *Our love's a quiet stream.*
For do you think such words make up to me
The raging torrents of a lovers' dream
That I have never known as you and he,
The one you gave the fever of your youth?
With gentle word, with smile, with cool caress,
With spoken love you think to hide the truth:
For him you throbbed, for me there's tenderness.
But stay. I can't demand what you can't give.
For how can I demand that anywhere?
And who am I to say you shan't relive
Your moments just because they're not to share?
Perhaps we've time to share one smaller dream
Here along this quiet homeward stream.

Ooo!

Welcome, said the kangaroo,
Welcome to our little zoo.
Solicitous, he wondered, too,
if yet perhaps the new gnu knew[1]
where water was and hay to chew.

---

[1] In my native Nebraska dialect, said to have been the preferred language of 800-numbers until Indian English usurped its claim, *chew, gnu, knew, new, too, kangaroo,* and *zoo* rhyme perfectly. Likewise, for me, *horse* and *hoarse* are sound-a-likes, as are *marry, Mary,* and *merry.*

Inner Weather

Snow on cedar boughs and birds bright red
And sky's own egg-shell blue domed overhead
And frosted breath at five degrees below.
Atop a neighbor-pine, sitting sentinel, a crow
whose coded calls bring answers from the grove
nestled in the wind-hushed cove
beyond this cedared hill.
How pure it seems, how sanctified, the chill.

Yes, so it seems, well-mufflered as I am
against the killing cold and knowing that the dram
and hearth await me in the hamlet far below this height,
far below but steady in my sight.
Imagine wandering, sun-forsaken, on this slope,
lonely, hungry, naked, and bereft of hope.

The World War I Dead Pass in Review

oh we died when the guns with the chatterbelt spoke
when the tanks crunched over and our fragile luck broke
with a last breath o' gas and a final hoarse croak
and the trench mud spattered what the bleeding didn't soak

but they said it was worth all the bleeding it brought
as they sat back safely where they couldn't hear a shot
it was peace that we bought and we'd surely we thought
be the last troop passing but we see that we are not

Black Sonnet

for the wood thrush

Hush!
Hear the southern silence; hear no thrush
carol: *ee-oh-LEE*
chee-CHEE
WHEE-irr.
Where oak and hickory were,
they stand no more,
in their stead, a littered street, a crackerbox, a liquor store.

Hear no thrush.
Rather, hale the rush
of trucks, breathing odious blessings on the air.
Everywhere,
in place of sacred groves are to be seen
the monuments to such as love another green.

From Here to Bryce[2] and Back

The tungsten trees wear well
in the two-mach slip of time.
Still, even they glow
and burn away. The lesson's lost,
if old ambivalence encrusts the grid.
And how is that to be escaped?

---

[2] *Bryce* is the state mental hospital for adults. Its campus lies next to the campus of the University of Alabama in Tuscaloosa, Alabama.

Brycelings come to mind, their hands
sticky with the chocolate of example. But that
won't satisfy you, will it? You demand
examples catatonic with rational
obsession. Well, then, you deserve
the institutions you're committed to.
Without due process of thought,
I concede, but the choice has been yours.

The quality of morning light's
another example. How else
are the dawning insights of birdsong
to be explained? At least, without
that old *reductio ad absurdum*?

I grant there's no right place
to close the tête-à-tête
of ancient confrontations. Nor
to open it. And how might it
be otherwise? How do facing mirrors
put bounds if not by their
bounded infinity? And, of course,
there it is: the old ambivalence.

You say I must say what makes sense.
But the lift stops thrice, at least,
above the catacombs. Who's
to say where sense steps in
or out? Precisely. The antidote, perhaps,
is frequent drafts of tickertape.

Have I marked how that giant shark
drifts against the sky-blue?
He's relevant, too; I take it
on faith. Though perhaps the stains
he spreads were best broached
another time in other neighborhoods.

The thread is broken, and knots
pull badly through these
mind-loomed swatches. Best
to start again, but one can't remember
where. Or how. Or even why?

The Church on the Hill

There he stood on the steps of the church on the hill
'Mid the corn and the hay in the fields that he saw
To the south, to the west, to the north, to the east,
And he looked to the east and a bit to the south
To the church in the vale but a mile or but two
From the steps where he stood and bore thoughts of what was:
The church here, white and wood, the church there, red and brick,
The church here on the land, the church there in the town,
In the town of his birth, in the town of his thoughts,
In the town with the church that was theirs and not his,
As the church on the hill was not theirs but was his;
The church here with its bell, the church there with its bells
That would ring out as one when the new year had come.

In his mind they rang now as they'd rung for the child.

To his right, to the south, close at hand lay the sod
Where they slept, those held dear in the thoughts he bore now.

In a time now long gone this was where he had come
From the town in the dale to this church on the hill
Where the winds had blown strong in both heat and in cold
When the snow lay in drifts on the sod where they slept,
The first ones who had come to this land, to this hill.

Now he stood as he had on the steps of the church
In the smile of the sun 'neath the blue of the sky
In the still of the wind in the fresh of the day,
And he thought of the past and of what was to come,
And it seemed both were good and it seemed both were right,
If he thought they were good and he thought they were right,
As he did as he stood 'neath the smile of the sun
And the blue of the sky and with noon yet to come.

But it seemed both were bad and it seemed both were wrong,
If he thought they were bad and he thought they were wrong,
As he might if bruised clouds palled the sky of his mind
And the noon was far gone and the dusk was at hand.

But then how could that be?
Could his thought make it so?
Could it be that to seem is the same as to be?
And he thought then of one who had thought that it might,
And he thought of the tale of the ten who were blind
And of how each would see what he thought he had felt.

In his mind he could see the ten men who were blind
And the Oz where they lived, how each thought to be wise.

Ah, but one of the ten was the one who could speak
And the rest would give in and the one was the one
Said the world was a wall or quite much like a wall.

So it came, for the length of his day in the sun
That the world was a wall to all of the wise.

But at last the one died with his day in the sun,
And one came who was sure that the world was a trunk,
Was the trunk of a tree and so sure of the truth
Was this one that the nine thought it wise to give in.

So it came, for the length of his day in the sun
That the world was a tree-trunk to all of the wise.

But at last this one died with his day in the sun,
And one came who was sure that the world was a snake,
And so sure of the truth was this one that the wise
Thought it best to give in.

So it came, for the length
Of his day in the sun that the world was a snake
To all of the wise.

But at last this one died
With his day in the sun, and one came who was sure,
And so on, and so on.

And the world?

It was still
What it was and had been, was a wall, was the trunk
Of a tree, was a snake, was a rope, was a fan,
Was a spear, was a this, was a that, and was these
All at once!

And was more than its parts, as had been
For all time.

So it was, thought the man as he stepped
From the steps of the church in the sun on the hill,
With the church in the dale that was theirs and not mine,
With the church on the hill that was mine and not theirs.

So it was with the good or the bad of the past.

So it is with the right or the wrong of the age
Still to come, and so on.

Yet it lurked there: a doubt.

As he walked on the sod past the stones with the names
Of his kin and the ones that they'd known and the ones
That they'd mourned, as he read on a stone

JETZT RUHT ER IN GOTT[3]

It was then that he thought that they might have been right.

And it came like a cloud on the sky of his mind
Ah! that time he had sat in the pew with his dad,
He, the son who'd come back from the world as it seemed
And his dad who was thin and was gray with his years.

So small the deed I might have done,
to stand with the man at his side in the pew
for old time's sake, for years of love,
of thought for the boy and not for the self,
to stand with him there in front of them all,
to take with him then the bread and the wine . . .
What had it hurt?

What!
I had called down the wrath of his God on my head?
What kind of half-a-faith was that?
Then had he gone in peace down to his grave.
Too late . . . Too late . . .

And so then let it be.
                                        Now he walks to his car
And goes back to the world that has seemed for so long,
Far, so far, from the church in the wind on the hill
That is his and is theirs and the church in the dale
That is theirs and is his but a mile or but two
From the steps where he'd stood and heard bells in the sun.[4]

---

[3] "Now he rests in God."

[4] Did you notice that this poem consists entirely of one-syllable words? Keep an eye out for others along the way. Easy? Try it!

The Quality of Light in Alabama

a bronze for Cash

. . . to heap them in redundant profusion one upon another
until meaning vanishes and there is nothing left
but the sweet, canorous drunkenness of sound,
nothing but the play of primitive rhythm
upon the secret springs of emotion

W. J. CASH, THE MIND OF THE SOUTH 51 (1941)

and even now, in this
the ready soul's season,

these oaks are leaved in leather
of wannest cheek and spirit

How can it be? you say,
and I tell you face to face,

with the brinksman's ultimate knowing,
in syllables old and fresh

as returning rain, about
the loss that saved us
                                        from what?

The mind wanders, a fuzzy
needle in the coke-sticky

valley of a golden oldy
And that's it, of course,

the gaunt and ivory what
from which the teller's tongue

recoils! There it stands,
feigning transparence in the long

rays of the tangent sun,
fragile in the too tactile

resonance of

And here again

the pantomime of old discon-

tinuities must stand in
for the newly brazen tongue

How fares? Why steals the scene!
And wouldn't you have known it!

Or would have had you thought
your way back along

the brink of old anxieties

•

The fall had been a riper
time to speak this, I agree,

but then, who's to say,
or who might have said,

when or whether (the leaves
that fluttered down here

seven woods ago
fluttering up again

to catch the dappled ghost
of sunsmile long ago

transfigured) that were possible?
The road not taken,

after all (a doctor's
thesis recently has shown

empirically), opens on
a billboard, winner of

the proudest prize bestowed
by the advertising counsel,

so I'm told
                    All this,
I think you'll agree,

bears with special force upon
the readiness of souls and,

to be precise, the likelihood
that seasons are to seemingness

even as the quality
of southern light
                              Have I said

how the dogwoods open their
wounded hands as if April

were theirs to give? Or how
the sleepless mockingbird,

fixed in the cold compassion
of the late and lonesome moon

bears fruit of a muse
never before acknowledged

in these latitudes? It
were best perhaps I didn't

Still, someone might hear,
might really, really hear,

as the beautiful box of the last
Stradivarius will hear (if hope

is more than desolation's
kinky whore) the teachings

of that ultimate long bow

•

But friends, you mustn't agree
if you think for a moment I speak

in other than the spirit of lucence
transfixing us all who wonder

under these skies. Perhaps
it's a kind of madness. Or

a certain luminous seeming
of plain, unwonderful things. Or

merely the ripening of time
under the southern sun.

Dialogue

Happy people don't write poetry, he said.
They write verse instead.
Poetry
is therapy,
whether you write it or read it.
If you're really into poetry, it's 'cause you need it.
Can we not foresee
Prozac could be the death of poetry?

And she: *Chaucer seemed a happy man.*
Prove me wrong, if you can
at this remove without your question-begging, pseudo-psychoanalytic tool.
It seems your proffered rule
is but
another way to say what's poetry and say what's not.

Hawthorne

Have I at last had done with all pretense?
Or will I somewhen hence
look back on what is now
and see another me I'll do my best to disavow?
Mask after mask I've thought the last
only to consign another to the past.
The light goes down. I've looked about as far as I can see.
Perhaps there is no *really me.*

Search forth? Is it worth the candle?
To know for sure . . . Would it be more than I could handle?
Trudge on.
Perhaps before the gloaming last is gone . . .
We'll see.
What if there is no *really me*?

On Reading Him Again in Later Life

How now! and *What!, i' faith,* and all the charm
Of English at its best, its happiest,
Deployed to teach a people how to speak.
He shook his inky spear, a feather's weight,
And all the sounds of English as it was
Fell to and had their day upon the fields
He staged for them upon imagined scenes
Of circumstance, exposed and tickled each
And every foible of the English folk,
Enamb'ring thus the substance of his Age.

Coole Park, 1998

A Gyre for Yeats

Well then!
Suppose you're right; suppose such days will never come again.
We'll hafta make these do.
True,
things won't seem quite as they seemed before.
Still, other seemings may become us more.
In any case,
grim default aside, we hafta run the race.

And count on this: Some day,
a younger they
will rue
the passing of *the glory days* we just made do.
See how the moon goes down full bright!
Have we, younger, ever watched through such a night?

Wind and Pines

The wind suggests.
The loblolly pines
say, *Yes.*
Not all at once.
The bright ones,
dawn-colored faces shining,
catch on first.
The others, behind them,
nod in turn
as they get the idea,
the very idea,
of picking up and moving on.
But rootlessness comes
much easier to the wind.

Pines learn it at their peril.
Once learned, there's no return.
And they know it.
Or perhaps inertia's easiest.
So they nod and say, *Yes,*
and sigh in envy of the wind,
the fancy-free, the rootless,
whispering thoughts of discontent.
But they stay, they stay,
sighing, *Yes, Yes* . . .

Horse and Rider

Rippling rider, shimmering steed,
on the galloping words of the wind they rushed,
overtaking the tumbleweed,
outrunning the gyring sodium dust

at the fluid brim of this waterless plain
between the outward and inward eyes,
now gone, now there, now gone again,
wraiths of this sulphurous paradise.

And lo! the beholder, who was he,
canister empty, tongue of brass,
becalmed on this conjured creosote sea
miraculous miles from the angels' pass?

Were he and the steed and the rider one
at the fluid brim of the barren past,
figment of the smithering sun,
rattling, *Water*, at the last?

Life Is Discovered on Another Planet

On that orb, in those days,
a few could see. The rest did not
believe in sight. What light
could be transformed to good for all,

for all! was mirrored, focused by the few
who could. Surely they were honored
then, these guardians of sight, these bringers
of blessings to all men? They lived

in fear, fear and silence, lest the blind
should hear that they were different and strike
them down for hate and spite. Thus,
it was: For many passings of the torch,

the few sustained the unbelieving,
the unwitting blind. For what reward?
Life. A certain satisfaction.
Too, what else was there to do?

Forever

"There will never be an end
To this droning of the surf."
Wallace Stephens, Fabliau of Florida

The sea
lavishes its energy
upon the shore
with constancy transcending metaphor.
Patient miller, milling stone to sand,
grinds the grist of ages on the strand
piece by crystal piece
without surcease.

Forever? No . . .
Even Earth recalls a long ago
without the sandy surf to craze her virgin stone.
And she alone,
her waters boiled away, will last abide
to greet her fate as galaxies collide.

Omen

8:45 a.m.
7.19.05
a doe
close, close by
below this kitchen window
stands among the flowers
by the bird-bath
nibbling leisurely
chewing thoughtfully
crossing the lawn
she puts them
dainty down, her toes
two by two, two by two
picks her way
beyond the lawn
behind a flowerbed
along the rail
before the brink
of the ravine
and disappears
below the brink
down, down toward
the trickle of the brook

The Nuns of the Antarctic

Twilight.
The nuns of the Antarctic stand upright
upon their floe,
giving praise in the only way they know.
Will such reverence suffice
to work their resurrection from this ancient ice,
drifting at last, free!
on the timeless essence of this sacred sea?

Believe.
It were sacrilege to grieve
for heaven's own
here at the very dome of heaven's throne.
See how joyously, at last, they leap
into the welcoming ice-blue deep.

What Beast

This is a test. This is only a test.
The center still holds. We're doing our best.
The thunder, the thunder, it's making us wonder
just what is coming from over yonder.

At ease, at ease, don't trouble your rest.
This is a test. This is only a test.
The rumble grows louder, it roars like a beast.
We fear we are doomed to be part of the feast.

The air is grown acrid the sky is grown gray.
Night's coming on and it's only midday.
This is a test. This is only a test.
Those who've denied it are under arrest.

And those who have not can no longer for choking
the cities are burning the country is smoking . . .
Doubters be curséd! Believers be blest!
This is a test. This is only a test.

Triumph in a Minor Key

I whetted my cruel crescent
Fanned the dull fires
Burning in the depths of my depthless sockets
Clutched my shroud about me
And went for him
I rattled at his door and entered
But when he saw 'twas I
He laughed
He laughed, and the harvest was bitter
And my homeward journey meaningless

The Night Before

Bleak watch
Loneliness
Ebon depths of heaven fathomless
Still

Crisp snow
Mirror ice
Silhouettes shivering in the frigid vise
Cold

Moonlight
Stars bright
Illuminated fleece and fallen white
Peace

Lamplight
Flickering fires
Glowing beneath huddled roofs and spires
Warm

Faint bells
Pulsing high
Tiny apparition flows across the sky
Doubt

Red form
Twinkling feet
Pairs of flashing branches crowning eight
No

Now here
Now gone
Miraculous and seen by only one
Mum

Analogies

Someone once said to me,
Sundown's the saddest time of day.
It haunts me with its wan analogy
to that near hour when life must fade away.

My friend, (I had to smile)
I like what you analogize.
For never sunset yet but in a while
Was followed by a lovelier sunrise.

Sonnet No. 1

When we were young, you'd not have looked at me,
And I as surely would have passed you by.
Perhaps you lacked that fatal chemistry,
The nectar that could keep bees buzzing nigh.
And I? Was I the sort of dashing drone
For whom the choicest flowers open wide?
No, I confess I often buzzed alone.
Then why are we content here side by side?
Is it because we now can recognize
Those treasures hidden from the rape of youth?
Or is it that we've learned to compromise?
But life has taught us not to seek such truth.
We'll cling with need's affection till we die,
Content that it is so, not asking why.

Odelet to Sex

Sex is the moment in focus
so sharp there is no dusk
to be, no dawn that was,
no breath of that ancient anguish
to sicken the palate's blush.

Sex is alone the power
(or word or deed be sure)
to press eternity's frontier
back, back from harvest's hour,
to ease that ultimate despair.

Banshee

Late at night,
when the wind is right,
that sound
drifts in from west of town:
the duet wail of a diesel train,
plying her trade come moon, come rain.
What treasures she brings she doesn't say,
or whether she spirits them away.

Some late-at-night,
when the wind is right,
I'll answer the call of that duet horn
in the wee-est hours of the coming morn.
Others will hear it, so they'll say,
spiriting, spiriting me away.

New Rome, Alas! As Paradise Re-Lost?

Far be it from my pen and from my Muse
To turn the Heavens upside down, or Earth,
Nor yet to call upon the Name of God
To serve ungodly ends as often do
The Power-Lusty and the Greedy-Rich,
Estranged from God, yet calling on his Name
As wolves will don the fleece to fleece the sheep
Or, worse, to bleed and turn them on the spit.
Nor do I have in service demagogues
To snare the innocent with webby words,
With sticky words to dangle them as prey
Before th'ascendant god, old Mammon known.
My Muse, alas! a child of her time,
Has never known to sing those ancient names,

Yet still she knows the Humpty-Dumpty tale,
How bad eggs claim their own reality,
Of Midas turning even God to gold.
How like the Sixteen Hundreds now! Forbid.
So where begin? With Eden lost again,
A chance perhaps now lost to greed and love
Of shrunken self, a chance to bless anew
Creation, yes, Creation even as it rings
Adown the ages in the many tongues
Of all the many tribes of Adam's get,
Partakers of That Certain Tree or not,
To go beyond the words of Adam Smith,
Abused these days to put the megamerchants
On the throne instead of Kings—or God?
Oh, tongue of Jeremiah, be my own
To warn the seeing and the blind about
The chasm ever-widening between
The Haves and Have-Mores mansioned on the cliff,
The high cliff, and the ever-poorer poor
Behoveled in the winds upon the low:
Ignorance and Want, as Christmas Present warned.
Attend! What hiss arises from the Yawn,
The Gullet of that gaping gash? What writhes
in dark so deep below we see it not?
Or them? Is it perhaps the Legions o'th' Damned?
In league at last with Chaos, Blackest Hole?
Oh, Ignorance and Want! Oh, Greed and Disregard!
Until the Good Lord's Desperate here on Earth
Like hordes of army ants engulf us all.
But more anon. Meanwhile, what óf that tree,
That Certain Tree, the one that's said by some
To be the cause of all our woe? What fruit
Has it borne since? Can we agree it was
No tree of Knowledge generally, but just
Of doctrine of a certain kind, that is,
One unexamined answer to a posed
Dichotomy that is no clear dichot-
Omy at all in any universal sense?
(Who disagrees should ask around the Earth
Just who Great Satan is.) That tree has borne

much bitter fruit; my Muse, let's let it lie.
    But let's bethink another kind of tree,
A Tree of Knowledge come to later fruit,
A Tree of Knowledge sensibly conceived.
What's *knowledge*? What dóes it mean indeed—to *know*?
This question stirs, has stirred, as much discord
As has the meaning óf That Certain Tree.
To *know* is not, when sensibly conceived,
The same as *take on faith*, that is, *believe.*
Believing is religion's word. *Knowing*
Belongs to *knowledge—Science*, in a word—
Not *faith*. And *faith* is not a way *to know*.
    No true scientist would disagree,
I think, that scientists, as seekers of
What Is, renounce the whimsy that they know
For sure, that is, for certain-sure, *What Is*.
That's not to say that certain reckonings
Do not from present evidence suggest
To "common sense" (whatever that may be)
That doubt's been laid to rest when 't comes
To this or that conclusion about fact.
That's just to say that we know less, much less,
For certain-sure than what we think we know.
Some facts-supposed we know for sure-enough
To act upon, what though not certain-sure.
(Like, were you there when "we" landed on the moon?
And yet, what action is required upon
Your "knowing" that? Supposing that it's so
Does not expose your life to risk, but just
Puts you in harmony with what your friends
And kin around you think—and that's a boon.)
Science, for true science' sake, assumes
The modesty of doubt, without which
Humankind would seek no more, as seek
It didn't ín a darker age, as seek
It won't again, if demagogues prevail,
If certain faiths impose an arrogance
Of certainty that calls the darkness back.
    Which brings us, as perhaps it must, around
To á most vexing discord óf our time

And place, my people-o. To wit:
The origin of species. Whénce wé?
True Science, science rightly known,
Suggests on present evidence, the kinds
We see, we hear, we taste, we smell, we touch,
We bear a pedigree of ancient birth,
Most ancient birth of worthy works of time.
Whether time will bear this inference out
True science cannot claim to say; unless
It cease to be itself, instead become
Philosophy or faith. And that is where
The shepherd-wolves come in: Bleating even
Louder than their sheep, they claim TO KNOW
Upon no evidence at all—at best,
On evidence neither science nor
The law can entertain and still be science,
Still be law. "So much for science," they say,
"And law must yield to holy writ." (Whose
Holy writ we do not have to guess.
Theocracy we aren't—yet. If you
Would see what our United States
Would be as á theocracy, but look ye
To Islam, Islam as practiced where it 'rose,
Where to believe in other than Islam
Can be your death—not just eternally.)
"So much for science," they say, or else: "We have
Our science, too: intelligent design."
Scientists, too, as philosophers, can muse
Upon intelligent design, but such surmise
Falls short of science, lacking rigor's proof.
It's possible (not likely, though) that stern
Research, the kind that science requires,
May someday ages hence give reason to suppose,
As tenable hypothesis, the thought
That sapient design's behind it all.
'Til then, intelligent design remains
And will remain what it is now: faith,
Not science, no, to that not even close.
Faith and science can reconcile, but mix
They can't, they mustn't, lest they both decay.

"So much for science," they say, "Scientists are not
By God (whose God we needn't ask) inspired."
What! Not by God (whoever's God) inspired?
Did this Intelligent Designer you
Propose make all or not? Or leave some part—
Let's say, the best of brains—to Lucifer?
And if this High Intelligence did make
The best of brains, how fails then that
Intelligence to sanctify their use,
To boast them as the best of the Design,
To bless them in their holy search to know
The will and craftsmanship of That which made
Them thus, and all the Universe besides?
What! The best and brightest but a snare
To trip the middling mind? Blasphemy!
T' impute such meanness, such deceit to One
Deemed loving ánd most just impugns all faith.
And still there's more to say against that Trojan
Wolf, intelligent design, than shepherds wolfish
Wish to hear or want their sheep to hear.
The wily worshipers of Smart Design
do not attain the square of their desire,
Unless we make with them that leap of faith
T' th'r special-pleaded, special-purpose god.
Yes, Christian sheep (and Christians in the main
are not such sheep) will make just such a leap,
And that their shepherd-wolves depend upon.
But Muslim sheep are good at leaping, too,
Although their cloven hoofs find other ground.
And, likewise, lead the leaps of Hindu sheep
And Buddhist sheep and sheep of other kinds
T' intelligent designers of their own
Design, their very own. And thus, the shepherds
Of competing flocks (that is, competing shepherds
Of the hapless flocks) do find themselves again,
Yea, once again, back at that square called one!
But woe, alas! their charges make the leap.
Upon this innocence of worldly sense
The wolves of worldliness play out their schemes.
Our polity is one of Oligarchs,

Disguised as a republic lied to be
Democracy!. (Think not? Do you know how
to say *Elect'ral College*?) Our Oligarchs?
None other than the Greedy Rich behind
The scenery and those, the Power Puppets,
who wily wield their will. (Think not? Bethink
The Elephant and how it tromps upon
Our hopeful garden plots. Bethink the Shrub
And how it sprang from soil manured with oil.)
Wily wolves! they talk the talk of faith,
Of troglodytic faith, but walk, nay, skulk
Most corporate, and, morsel-wise, they do
Most gormandly incorporate the sheep
Brought tó them by the Judas demagogues.
And not just those so (rightly?) brought,
But all the rest of us-not-powerful.
  Meanwhile, around the world, its poorer parts,
See how our baleful Christianity,
Our most ungodly stance on birth-control,
Has blasted any hope of better lives.
Oh, may we, ín our sleep, see babies damned
To blisters, scabs, and suff'ring worse than death.
See how their little bellies bloat, how flies
and death do swarm about their starving mouths,
and they but weeks or months or scant years old.
How's that more merciful, less evil, than
Alternatives? Oh, demagogues! your one
And only hope at Judgment Seat lies here,
The plea: *Forgive! We knew not what we did.*
  And all the while, our poets, those in power,
Play their fiddles while the naked starve
And cities burn. You, sitting sipping tea
Behind your window, sleek and warm, see you
No poem i' their eyes, the hungry, sick, and cold?
Can you say *roaches, rats, lead-paint*?
Can you say *lie*, can you say *cheat* and *steal*?
Can you say *underpay* and *overreach*?
Can you say *hopelessness* and *peace-be-damned*?
Are we the feeling ones, the ones who care,
Who call our ingrown smugness poetry?

And you! ye factious, fractious of a faith,
Is not your smug belief there are no rooms
For those of other faiths in Heaven's House
mean-spirited? Judge not! Lest ye be judged.
Oh, ye of every faith, of any faith, or none,
Bow down to Whom or What you will, but know
Your deities, however named, are one,
One w' th' the God of every tribe, the God
Of every place, the God of every time,
However named. But grant the boon *you* wish
To *all* and live! in hope that it will be
Untó you, évery óne, accórding to your fáith.
I've had a dream, again, again the same.
It comes from Her, my Muse, I do believe
(Although she may be prompted from above).
I see Her standing on a cloud, a cloud
Above our Mother Earth with all the wounds
Inflicted by accursed mánkind on hér
And ón her progeny, the innocent.
I hear Her sing (I know, Herself's a she):
Uplift all Womankind (submission plagues
The Earth); but teach Her self-support, but grant
Her dignity, let Her control Her own maternity,
And see how Eden's breezes stir again.
She sings, as well, of other healing tunes;
Of Martin's dream; of true enlightenment
That glares on pied and purchased pipers;
Of knowledge, food for thought, for all who take
And eat, such nourishment as they can well
Digest, and all according to their need.
And see how Eden's breezes stir again.
Will we give ear? Will we call our better
Genius forth? (Our record's not so good.)
Do we, enough of us, have love enough
For progeny we'll never know,
Yes, even down to children's children's heirs,
To leave a better world to them than we
Inherited? (So far it seems not so.)
Shall the shepherd-wolves who pipe us now
Deceiving melodies deceive us still,

The innocent, the willful blind, or will
We teach ourselves and, yes, our lambs, to cease
Repaying them, the shepherd-wolves, for fond
Diversions ánd for foolish self-esteem
With wool, and what is worse, with mutton chops?
(The wolves, I fear, will not agree our schools,
Their schools, should teach such mutiny.
That would be, to them, most awkward for
Us sheep to know, that liberating light,
Class-consciousness.) If we cannot so vote
ourselves to power, or if the shepherd-wolves
Cannot repent and bring themselves to study
Greed no more—and war, cannot be born
again into a life (oh, foolish hope!)
Of truest shepherdry like that of One
They preach to us, then woe! then woe! to us
And those, our seed, who follow us in next
And generations hence. Yea, they will curse
Our memory, as we ourselves have cause
To curse our dead, the generations past
Who left us—oh, so black bequest—with war,
With slavery, with all the rest those wraiths,
The Horsemen, bring us ín their baleful train.
How like the Sixteen Hundreds now! Forbid.
    New Rome! New Rome! which will it be: Greed
Deified and "laissez faire"? Eden
Lost—again? Or more heavenly Home on Earth?
Answer! Answer![5]

---

5 Chances are you've recognized this piece as a John Milton knock-off.

Another Theory of Poetry

Why the poemy line
for prosy thoughts? Well,
it's easy on the eye
and light to the touch.
It's fun to write this way,
light and lifty,
like loping downhill
in the face of a fresh breeze.
Assuming no shortage of paper,
it can at least be said
to counterpose no harm,
so the benefits needn't be weighty.
It reflects the plan of the cosmos,
being mostly space
with occasional peppers of substance.
And it's what I can do.
If I can't sell it,
I'm out of luck,
Actually, it's—as they say—
the REE-yal thing.

Each of us:

a momentary message
from past to future

Oh, Moon,

Listen to your ravished sister, Earth.
Do not surrender to his first adventurous kiss.
Don't be seduced by scientific manners.
See how he's already left his rash upon your breast.
Don't get pregnant with his misbegotten progress.
Say, *No*. Say, *No*.

The Rains of November

Remember the rains of November?
How they strolled in the woods like
the moccasined souls of first inhabitants,

playing their steady, revolving
rhythms on fallen pages
of another year? *How could I forget?*

you say, conjuring images
I wouldn't recognize.
And who's right? No matter,

perhaps, so long as disparate
visions do converge
in what we share: the cold

rain drenching down
through the roofless pillars of groves,
hallowed by subsequence; a gray

squirrel on a branch, wet-
black, pretending sunshine,
turning the red dogwood

berry in precocious hands;
the light, when the western edge
of the quilted cloud turned

up, as if the gods were peeking
lustfully under the covers.
Is that what we share? you say.

You speak again in tongues
I still must take on faith.
And do. Forsaking the vain

precision of assent, we touch
in constant celebration of our troth.
The rains of November, don't you see,

are an anchorage whereon our lonesome
vessels rise and fall
in a certain semblance of communion.

New Cartridge for Wedding Pen (12.30.71)

Such a fine writing tool!
And I yearn to write
fine things.
But fool
that I am I might
as well wish for wings.

Two Bunnies for Fum

Á ma femme, who asks why I can't
just write about bunny rabbits.

In the clearing, two rabbits,
moon-silver inlay in the emerald night,
dance a ritual pas de deux
from memory without event.

Are there words? A chant?
All lean to hear. The night
grows crystal quiet, strangely leer[6]
of pine murmur and frog lament.

The gnomes of silence
speak of snapping twigs;
silver rabbits wash across the night,
wispy wakes fading into doubt.

The tall pines breathe again,
and then,
voice by voice, the listeners ask
what the happening was about.

Who knows

whom our descendants will proclaim?
And will it matter to the shades of those
Proclaimed? Who of them will need it, this acclaim?
These sleepers of the blessedest repose?

---

6 An Old English word meaning *empty*.

Rise and Fall

From what then came to pass, move on.
A tale it is of time long gone,
a time of wind and snow, deep snow,
when wolves, dire wolves, were on the go.
Elk heard and elk feared,
when pines hushed and wind veered.

Huts loomed in woods, swart woods and deep,
that held a wild folk in keep.
The dark of speech swept forth to raid
and rape the land where sun's light played.[7]
Time passed. A time came
when old sun struck new flame.

From what has come to pass, move on.
What makes us think this fire the dawn,
when wolves gorge of as dire a kind
and we are prey and we are blind?
Wolves, Hear! and Wolves, Fear!
when pines hush and winds veer.

---

7 That is, on the Roman side of the Rhine and Danube Rivers

Happy Anniversary

He chuckled
sitting leg on leg at ember pit
mouthing meaty bone like bass harmonica
watching comrade shaggy as himself
chip another mark in unhewn wall.
Know what day this would have been?
No answer but the grate of rock on stone.
This would have been the day
the heirs of power
opened the time capsule.

All the Difference

The mockingbird and his song are one,
without mediation of will,
as he sings his song.
He doesn't think, *I'm singing*,
or, *I will make this sound.*
While it lasts,
his song is part of him,
his momentary neurochemistry.

The man and his thought are one,
without mediation of will,
as he thinks his thought.
He thinks, *I am thinking this thought,*
and, *I will this thought.*
While they last,
the thought,
the thought of thought,
are part of him,
his momentary neurochemistry.

Return of the Native 1

So, my stabled beasts, you do not speak
as legend says, and the midnight appointed's upon us.
How I, the child, marveled and the tingle spread,
as the elders spoke of your enspiriting. No,
no, low and nicker weren't meant.
(Hear the bark, deep in the throat, of the snow-
wind, how it nuzzles the brave barn, sturdy
as good memories, softened and silvered by time,
searches out vainly the way in.) But you
shall have this re-enacting, this ancient ritual
of farmer fathers (I so long the peregrine prodigal
bearing homage from afar), these measures
of good grain, prairie hay, and golden
straw beyond husbandry, the overbrim
of gratitude for blessings too much of the spirit
to be clearly said, and alas, to whom . . .

How the tackle creaked in the turkey-tail
that August day, the salt taste trickling
down the creases of a brown cheek, and these
great talonfuls of hay, bearing still
now in the poignant chill of December dream
the summer breath of virgin prairie hillocks
and freshly turned swath, tumbled down
together to await this moment of sacred
offering: whisper of the seeking snow; shudder
of stout timbers of hope against the buffeting
of wan alternatives; patient stir of comforted
creatures in the bountiful gift of golden straw;
sacramental breathing, partaken and bestowed
again in spirit envisioned and made visible
at this enchanted striking of the hour. And now
I know, the ancient fathers speaking certainly
across that vastest sweep of white, in voices,

though, most small here in silence
thus adorned: low and nicker were plainly
meant, if not so plainly spoken . . .

So, my stabled beasts, I leave you
to your silence and your speech; step out again
into that breach, that void, which I shall find
in time my medium, with hope, good hope,
that once again (holding the warm hand
of this most magic season, steps laid down
in child's faith, one upon another, through
a holiness of snow surpassing all the ancient
legends of the tribe) I'll see appear in brilliant
crystal aureoles of prophecy fulfilled the warm
and promised light . . . .

Epitaph 1

I could have done better,
I could have done worse.
And that's the end
of my little verse.

Invoking the Muse

Laddy, it's true,
the Muse is no one's constant companion.
Too, she doesn't come when called
and shows disdain for invitations.
But, Laddy, even granting this,
you've no excuse to fold your mind and wait.
Think *anything*. Put it down as if it *were* something.

Putting it down's like baiting a trap.
She sees you there, head bowed, as it seems,
in grand, ecstatic labor, and can't suppress her curiosity.
Soon she's looking over your shoulder and then,
with luck, she can't forbear suggesting something
here and there. She may even conceive it her own
and there you are, blessed and bemused,
the putative parent of another masterpiece.

Pilgrim

Whither, my friend, with tears
While others smile
It's yet a while
Till you must count your years

Why have you journeyed west
But faced the east
And valued least
What others deem the best

Whom do you look to greet
With glance so free
And fervently
Cast upon all you meet

What rhythm do you hear
That you can yet
Be out of step
With those who pass so near

Whither, my friend, and whence
'Twas, I surmise
A paradise
If told by your countenance

Two Wise Men

Two wise men countered thoughts one night
Of dying men and rays of light
They clashed on God's and nature's law
And on the verity of straw

I'll prove my straw's eternal truth
Said the older one, Forsooth
Explain away, friend, will you then
That straws are clutched by drowning men

The other: I concede the law
A drowning man will clutch a straw
And even though he knows it's vain
But which of them does that explain?

Vegas

The gods of odds enticed me
into consciousness to play
a friendly game with them.
The stakes were all the joy
that I could feel
and all the pain that they
could quill me with from void to void.

They dealt the cards,
and by my face they saw
the house would win again.
It evens out, they said,
Last apogee some guy got all the aces.
You're lucky, though.
It's worse to get a hand that almost wins.
I nodded foolishly.

I'd throw in now if I could play again,
but this will be my only hand.
So I might as well just play it out.
And, what the hell, the chips were free.

Of Catalysts

Who in heaven added that worthless catalyst?
I'll have his wings and halo!
(By creation, even Lucifer sinned no sin like this.)
The formula that I devised was finely weighed,
evolving with kaleidoscopic majesty.
Then some fifth-column son of the black angel
dropped that new synthetic in the tube!
It's in my image? That odd configuration
of wasted energy? It might improve my formula?
Get it out of there!
I know, I know, it won't be there for long,
but it's already altered my design.
The scheme will not unfold as I had planned
unless I intervene again.
My image? In a tempest's eye!
I'll have that helper's halo!
Someone neutralize that crazy catalyst
before it catalyzes everything!
If I should have to start from scratch again
I'd never finish this experiment
before lunch.

Winter Sundown in Alabama

They marked it well how he,
the prophet of disorder,
came nonetheless to poignant harmonies.

The season was right for it.

The orb's shadow, bending in space,
bent space itself to thinkable conformity.
Thingness melted to the touch of living light
through amber lucence towards intangiblest abstraction.

Even the dogs on that ethereal plane
barked silently through wrinkled time.

No wonder this could be, now
in spite of old discrepancies,
the timeless currency of equivalence!

Dial the wave-lengths off the present scale,
said he, *and this world disappears.*
Whether, imperceptible, it's there,
learnéd friends, brooks your inquiry at other leisure.
The point now is:
It seems that, once we rule against
the theories of omniscience,
we must see, willed or no,
that other worlds may occupy
this very space and time.

His was a mathematics
in which *x* was known,
a quantity domed and blue,
transposing innocent images pared to simplest principles,
stick persons clad in geometry;
great cities symboled in the fallible span of a single eye;
the unknown seen in a pale projection,
penumbral, unfocused, of the known;
cubed islands of intensest sanity, focused to the laser point of madness.

And now we see, said he, *the ancient savages spoke true.*
Begotten by the father's energy, conceived upon the mother's amplitude,
we are parented of sun and earth.
This amber light, this ambient broth,
these perfect pines radiant in their own incandescence
are life and the very stuff of spirit.

All this being true in some sense they couldn't penetrate,
they took their leave of contemplation,
accepted dissonant perceptions,
nothwithstanding they had marked it well of him

Head Stones

What! Three feet six by six I should claim
to bear the name
I bore
in the blink before?
And what thereafter?
Would it not be the laughter
of Futility,
that gremlin of a deity?

Better it were to evanesce,
not so?, to bless
the living poor with one more garden spot
to feed their hunger, ease their lot?
Ah, but the greedy rich, I rue,
would snatch that from the hungry, too.

Miraculous . . .

how the sun comes up just for us
no matter who, no matter where.
There's a lesson there . . .

Advice to One Better Off Than I

Why brood
because they gave you bad reviews?
The news
is that you've been reviewed!

To Name Shapes

One by one
the thoughts he thought
became the fame
of others.
Yet
he wasn't robbed.
Not his,
the thoughts.
They had, it seemed,
ubiquity,
own essence,
presence, currence,
implicity in all,
though still unseen,
till beaconed by a phrase:
giving shape
by giving shape
a name.
Not his,
the phrase, the fame.

Surviving the Century

Well, ol' Phoenix, here we are again!
This pinch of sodium ash seasons
the tongue with too familiar savor.
There's nothing for it, though, but
thp! thp! spit it out and head
for hearty water. The word our
previous renaissance was *keep on
keepin' on.* Whatever it is now,
we'll learn to say it, and will say it,
even knowing as we do for us
it's flammable. Trotzdem!
He won't be much who fears
too much to make an ash of himself.
We, ol' Bird, we know from sad
experience, are kindled easily. So
it's on once again with the courage
of one who has no choice
to the pinnacle—if only of pyres.

Picnic on the North Rim

No crumbs for us
They seldom taste like cake
and often like the fingers of the feasters
and the grit around their heals
Hungering we turn away
and wander off to forage for ourselves
to taste the dust that seasons bitter leaves

Still hungering we turn toward the rim
and shout encouragement across the void
Then when the echoes speak to us of hope
follow wistfully until at last
we teeter on the anvil's point
We contemplate the down, down, down
and try the splatter on for size one heartbeat long
Then grope-step toe and heel along the brink
that coming we could see but now must sense

The spiny grass hooks welcome anchors in our shins
the voices from the tables call again
The echoes from beyond the anvil drown
in peals of finger-licking mirth
We hear the laughter of the happy ones
a crippled meadowlark whose rumpled wing
and painful flounder-flight from bush to boulder
bring our numb hearts leaping back to life
It tempts us further, further from the nest
then leaves us mouthing feathers once again

Still hungering we turn toward the rim
and shout encouragement across the void
Then when the echoes speak to us of hope
follow wistfully until at last
we teeter on the anvil's point
Again the voices from the table call
We hear them growing fainter as we fall

In Praise of Fame

How apt that fame
should rhyme with name.
How odd that it
should rhyme with game.
The name lives on;
the game is done.
What use is fame?
It saves no one.

At the Capstone:[8] *Six Lectures to Look Out the Window By*

I

Describing the perceived
best describes the witness.
Its worth as description
of that perceived is at best
incidental and not to be trusted
as foundation of empires.
Then how must it stand with
our description of
our perception of the witness?

---

[8] That is, the University of Alabama, Tuscaloosa, Alabama.

II

Thinking
the individual
is important
is important
not because
the individual
is important
but because
thinking so
is important.
(If you follow.)

III

The poem lies in the eye of the beholder.
Thus, the beholder statures his eye
by knowing what statured eyes
behold these days and then
beholding that, too, or saying so,
and the two may really become one.

IV

Is it, after all, personality for sale?
Squiggles of evidence of a force worth knowing,
deep, deep in the labyrinth?
One had hoped for more: paradise found,
a womb of universals, essences.
Ah, well. Cup the small candle,
glow pathetic against the flash of mass display,
from the wash impelled by concussion of applause.
Someday, somewhere, someone
may grope and peer and be glad
to see from palm to palm.

V

It takes this or that chemistry to be this or that.
A feeling of choice is also requisite.
A range of formulae compels a range of beings
hard to justify. *Erratic,* we say, *Inconsistent.*
Being an ***I*** is not like being the weather.
The parameters of granted change are set like granite chins.
Rain too often and a certain kind of desert flowers about the foot.
Cracks appear. The pedestal crumbles.
Still, being is at least *a* reason for being.
Perhaps *the,* though feeling so requires a certain chemistry.

VI

Not from time to time the change, but from mood to mood.
Thus, from time to time only as mood moves in time,
or as mood as a measure of change is a measure of time.
Thus, does change, itself the measure, the meaning, of time,
appear to happen in time from time to time.
So, change is time; mood is time.
Thus, is mood change, and change from mood to mood
is change from time to time
The resonance, you see, may go on forever,
whatever that means in a world where change is time.

Right and Wrong

Doe's had the good fortune to suffer the right kind of wrong.
He'd had an oh-well kind of life until it came along.
Now he suffers on stage.
Now he's quite all the rage.
It's a state of affairs that he may even wish to prolong.

Roe's had the misfortune to stand for the wrong kind of right.
The Lefties and Righties assail him by day and by night.
It's just not in fashion
to channel one's passion
in causes more subtle than causes in black or in white.

Which Witch?

And today! Today!
Which witch does she play?
Broom or womb?
Poisonous apple or prick of the loom?
Kiss or curse?
One or the other for better or worse?
Enchanting words or *ee hee hee*?
Come closer, dear, and we shall see?

Ah, the witch from the other way,
who wields a wand that sprinkles day!
The witch whose bewitching tinsels dreams,
who sweetens *what is* with a pinch of *what seems*!
Beware, beware, what seems to bless!
It's all enchantment nevertheless!

Babel

Exalt ye then
thy faltering steps
toward Heaven?
Know ye not
thy steps are built
on the ruins of walls
strewn on the rubble
of towers?

On a Picasso I've Never Found Again

One begins with a face, sketched on a lower quadrant of the mind.
One stays the hand lest cumulation bend event to other issue.
Succeeding strokes, of course, are silent.
Faith alone discerns the staked perimeters.

This fear to profane the perfect has left us with those lines,
those strokes, that consonance and dissonance,
bequeathed by names who sought and were content
with that which would suffice.
We see them held before us nonpareil.
And so they are, in the glitter of that quotidian light
which shatters on the planes of its dimension.

The gods are not to be compared
who loom in that ether of veils beyond sound,
beyond sense,
beyond imagination.

Harvest Moon

You come to me and hold me close, and I hear
the wisdom of seasons of sorrow but happy seasons, too,
whispering maybe you can't bear
to share in words, I couldn't bear to know in words, the secret moving you,
but I've not told you either, and I won't, I can't,
what memory throbs in my throat just now,
shouldn't tell you, and I sha'n't,
what moves me to love you more than just anyhow.

What communion is this that, saying nothing, says I understand
what you mean to say by saying nothing as you touch my hand?

This is the speech of having endured,
having come to that season of frost and pumpkin moons
wherein Mays of promise, long immured,
lie weathered into wistfulness, along with hopeful Junes,
withered as if plain fact's freckled face
had frowned down like a spiteful sun
from glaring, whited blue devoid of any trace
of shade, wherein mocked, betrayed, undone,
what's left of victory seems withered compromise.

Come, hold me still. *What is* is all, *what was* is not:
We've won, if but in silence we will name the prize.

Such a Little Prayer

Let me move through the sweet grass
with the warm-eyed animals.
Let me not be green-eyed, cold-eyed.
Let me be a twig that snaps,
a breeze that whispers water.
Let me be the milky meadow fragrance
reminding you of warm-eyed creatures
grazing now beyond the knoll.

How Many Wars Can Dance on a Pin?

A war is waged and never won nor lost
The battlefield alone betrays the cost
The silent regiments in silence fight
A soundless battle in eternal night

⇳

And as the months of blackness wander by
The battlefield alone must bleed and cry
New forces join the siege and wage with might
But fight alone against both left and right

⇳

No allies here to tip the scales of fate
Contenders only stir the broil of hate
And as the years of turmoil build and blend
Only the battlefield has wounds to mend

⇳

What watching mortal would not quail to see
The bold destroyers' immortality
The victors fall, the fallen rise again
To slay in turn the slayers of the slain

⇳

And what contender needs to fear this war
When just the battlefield must bear the scar
The battlefield itself at last succumbs
And with it fades the throb of silent drums

⇳

The indestructible have been destroyed
Stilled with the field whereon they were deployed
And still there is the never-ending night
And somewhere in the dark another fight
Secreted away from sun and sight

Soliloque Anonyme

Thrasher, tell me,
why do you recite
more modestly
than your wordy cousin,
Mockingbird?
Because you lisp?
You do, you know.
It's no secret.

Or badly kept.
And yet, I tell you,
your shy soliloquy,
unauthored as it seems,
or else by the heart
of the leafing woods,
has made me pause,
scythe poised,
among the briars,
and rejoice
at what you say.
You rephrase the world
and I find
peace in the phrase
and meaning in the moment.

Love in the Afternoon

A needle-sharp pen-
cil and a virgin
page make me tremble
to be about it.
Too often, though, the
occasion rises
above me and I
wilt before it and
nothing gets begot.

Seasons

It seems a stronger season
of the soul: the spring bubbles
a birth of ratable flavor.

Still, to compare too avidly
inflicts budded wounds.

Ever the alchemist of metaphors,
the personal he remains
apprenticed to vision's revisions.
How else might it have been?
The pup pursuing the bounced
ball might have wolfed,
it seems, at the first throat.
Pieces glued might
instead have swept out.

The train, thoughtlessly arrived,
freightlessly departs, certainly
the turntable's darling,
the asterisk of sequence.
But who is sure of more
in the world of the emperor's clothes?

Now and then, it's true,
a sweetness remains that after
all may count for all.

And if the rest is blooming
crystals of interlocking
insignificance,
why come now,
good compadre, who's
to begrudge it? And to whom?

December: The Sun Sets Beyond Northwood Lake

Ever the Narcissus
of pools of living light,

the personal he
finds much to love

in deepest contemplation
of nature's seven veils

of chaste dimension.
How world's within

the world supposed,
confounding all the most

necessitous perceptions,
pursue exuberant orbits

nonetheless
upon those mandatory

emanations, alike
the ordering word and gravity

of the revolutions of his reason,
tickles his well-strummed

fancy, quite harmoniously,
to high regard for that

eternal, cosmic other,
that is, for himself.

Sly solipsist!

·

And if, after all,
everything appears,

or seems to appear,
as it would have to be

in a world of necessitous sense,
why what is that to him,

osmotic beneficiary
of pools of living light?

Solipsism

the self knows
can only know
the self
flashes pictures
of its self
on all phenomena
without the self
calls what it sees
truth, reality

Moth

I fluttered, fluttered 'round the flame.
It fascinated, drew me near.
But often as it called my name,
That often I recoiled in fear.
⇳

I could not seek the flower's dew,
Could not ascend too near the clouds.
And yet, I feared to flutter through
The scorching wall, the blinding shrouds.

⇳

Who knows what glory in the flame?
Who knows what worlds beyond it lie?
Does it temper butterflies or maim
and leave them wingless there to die?

⇳

Who knows what nectar in the flower,
What ecstasies wait high above?
For I have fluttered out my hour,
The time I had so little of.

⇳

Exhausted now I fall and lie
Between the two, the hot, the cool,
And, knowing neither one, I die,
A special wingéd kind of fool.

This Old House

It leans toward the road.
Would it, too, take its leave,
as did those whose last abode
it was, and grieve?

They, too, grew gray and blasted,
grew grayer and were gone.
The old gray house has lasted
and lingers on.

Without a word, it tells us
of what must surely come,
what mortal dread impels us
and leaves us dumb.

Jove, keep this weathered witness.
Through time as fast as light,
Let it hold fast its itness
'Til comes the night.

Libido

Doddering desire
fans no fecund fire.
Faithful, equal hand, Ah, Harry!
come, tarry
here with me!
Help me entertain most merrily
these maidens of the mind.
I don't get on so well with any other kind.

And if such dalliance leads
to satisfaction of my humble needs,
why then
I'll call upon the paper dolls again
sometime. But not too soon.
Mine is a waning, not a waxing, moon.

Autumn at Taos

fire on the slopes
raging up-ravine
through Douglas fir
'round granite fist
and oyster crust
combustible September
inflammable October
wispless aspen-fire
flame-dappling the green

running to the wind
around the wind
shimmering independent
in the wind
invincible by rain or calm
quenched by November
sullen gray

Freight Train

rolling and
wailing a-
long thru the
night thru the
timber the
bottom
by pastures and
plowing 'cross
rivers on
trestles and
highways at
crossings thru
villages
living and
villages
dying with
throat that is
warning with
throat that is
mourning a-
long by the
winking of
eyes that are
red and the
waving of
arms made of
steel without

hands unat-
tached to a
head that are
holding back
beadwork of
cars that are
waiting whose
drivers are
yawning and
hearing the
throbbing of
rollers on
railings with
blaring of
radios
full inter-
mingled and
thoughts of the
journey the
goal and the
welcome that
look with the
shining of
lights that are
quickened by
forces as
subtle as
those that en-
liven the
masters of
engines the
masters of
autos the
masters of
crossings who
watch as the
lantern that
swings on its
hanger is
smaller and

fainter who
listen to
rolling and
wailing get
fainter as
lights without
current go
fainter and
fainter as
breath in the
body goes
fainter and
fainter the
rolling and
wailing are
fainter and
fainter
rolling and
wailing
fainter and
fainter
rolling
wailing
fainter
fainter
fainter

Sonnet No. 2

When I was young, I revelled in my lust.
I tallied kisses and collected flowers.
I nurtured faith and then betrayed the trust
that offered buds and petals, nestling bowers.
And thus I raced with ever-reaching time
With some vague thought of beating it somewhere,
Of wringing every pleasure from my prime,
And gave no thought to those who seemed to care.

The ones who cared have long since looked aside,
And I'm no more the sort of dashing drone
For whom the choicest flowers open wide.
I'm welcomed by one tallied rose alone,
Her nectar long since robbed, her petals stressed,
But I am tired and need a place to rest.

Pallid Light Dapples the Shadows

There's been a shootin'—or a shootin' at.
Well, see, Foy was comin' home
Over the dam in his old pickup
When he seen this nigger, see,
This nigger kid, fishin' in the lake,
And Foy, he stopped like a good member should
'n' says, *You a member?*
No fishin' 'thout you a member
Or has permission (an' who the hell
Goin' permit a nigger kid?)
An' this kid, he says,
Uppish as you please, perfec' English
'n' all like he some smartass Capstone creep,
I HAVE PERMISSION, SIR,
An' this white kid,
Son o' that p'fessor, y'know
—lives where Ollie
Useta 'for he got foreclosed
'n' had t' move back downtown
'n' get his kids bussed—says,
THAT'S RIGHT, HE'S MY GUEST.
Well, I guess no guest
Never got no welcome like that before.
You know Foy, he ain't made payments
Over his head out here these past eight years
T' be sassed now in his own back yard
by no niggers ner lovers.

One thing led to another. There was shoutin'—
Foy first, sure, but the boys, too—
Them painted-on manners run in the rain—
An' the college kid—his folks is from here, too
—don't know what went wrong—
An' you know Foy, he run outta words
'Fore they did an' he ain't gonna lose
So he says, *You shootin' off yo' mouths perty good,*
Well I got me sump'm better to shoot off,
An' he runs back to his pickup
'n' grabs his rifle outta the window
'n' zings a few past their ears.
They heard their mommas callin'
An' that was all. Hope so anyhow.
Reckon we c'n hush it.

Bees

I am nothing
without the swarm.
It nurtures me. It gives
my being shape.
It lets me be;
that being so,
it cannot let me be.
I owe it all,
must give it all
that it, that I,
may be and be.
I give, and what I give
I get. The giving,
too, is mine.
The gift, the giving,
it, and I, are one.
Together, it is ours to be;
sundered, not to be.

Nativity

December's on the move. In the folds
of its gusty robes it holds
my forebears' holy season.
Can they lie down together, faith and reason?
Hear it, winter, high in the bony trees?
The furry shiver and puddles freeze.
The light within, without, so wan.
Where has my inner Christmas gone?

The snow, the snow's begun to fall
Is willed belief belief at all?
The hearth waits somewhere down below.
Have I lost all hope in the swirling snow?
Will I find my way home from this whiting dream?
Is it only the gift of belief can redeem?

Foreword

Where's the merit in this wordwork
by an author they ignore?
No one's put these sounds together
Ever quite like this before.
Of all the words that could be joined,
before this moment these were not.
Though man's been thinking now for ages,
never this melange of thought.
If familiar things around us,
if the ones that we hold dear
have their special meaning for us
just because we find them here
in combinations never matched

in present, past, or time to come,
surely we can prize this wordwork
in the same way, though it's dumb,
dumb and freckled like a cousin
whom we treasure nonetheless,
shapeless, too, and none too pretty
like the aunt we love the best.
Of all the gods of odds might show us,
we'll see less than we might hope.
We'd be prodigal to miss
one twist of their kaleidoscope.
Even though Now's critics slight it,
burning it can't make much sense.
Maybe someone else will like it
other generations hence.
Who are we to play the censor
to a Now we'll never know?
Maybe we should let the future's
children deal the fatal blow
or elevate with tap on shoulder
and the words, *I dub thee ART*,
the armored word that, once an urchin
begged for smiles at the start.

The Hands Above the Cloud

One must look with an inward eye
to see the hands above the cloud.
The lambs on the meadow come naturally,
dancing, dancing in the green sunlight,
to a rhythm of their own, or not their own.
The hands draw the cloud across the sun;
the wings of the shadow enfold the lambs.
The watchers of the outward eye
put their hands together for the lambs.
The watcher of the inward eye
puts his hands together
for the hands above the cloud.

The cloud withdraws, or is withdrawn.
One looking with the outward eye
sees wolves in the white, white snow,
dancing, dancing on the meadow,
pas de deux et trois in the blue-white sunlight,
a choreography of their own, or not their own.
The hands draw the cloud across the sun,
or it draws itself across the sun;
the wings of the shadow reclaim their wolves.
The watchers of the outward eye
acclaim the wolves. The watcher, the other one,
acclaims the hands above the cloud.

The hands above withdraw the cloud,
or it draws itself aside,
the wings of the shadow unfold, and lo!
the lambs on the meadow, in the ice-blue snow.
The jaws of the shadow yawn, and lo!
the wolves on the meadow in the purpled snow,
dancing, dancing around the jerking lambs.
The glare-grey sky fades behind the cloud.
The watcher, his outward eye,
regards the watchers, the others,
putting their hands (unwillingly?) together
for the lambs? the wolves? the purpled snow?
His inward eye, his very inward eye,
sees the hands above the cloud,
not resting though the cloud is drawn,
keeping the wippens dancing, dancing.

And still, though the cloud is drawn,
the hands above the cloud don't rest.
The watcher of the inward eye applauds,
applauds the lambs, the wolves,
applauds the choreography, the purpled snow,
applauds the hands above the cloud.
And then, the hands above the cloud do rest.
The light goes down: white, blue, purple, softest black.
The lights come up.

Ho, you non-writers,

reaching for a star,
to history
you'll only be
what writers
say you are.

Entry in a Diary

Two Fifteen 'Seventy-Six:
I burned the brush-pile today,
the one down on the orchard lot,
the one that's been there since early last summer
that I forgot to burn for a week or two
and then thought I'd better not,
because there might be thrashers in it, or wrens.
So I burned it today, before they were nesting again.
The fire fed on the fire till it roared in its throat,
and I thought of Hamburg and storms of flame,
riding their own high winds.
I looked, disquiet awax, up and around at the woods,
mine and the neighbors.
I wished I had brought more help
than a tarp and a rake.
I thought of Frost in his poem, fighting his fire,
winning at last, weary with effort and fright,
but light with the having won.
Mine didn't spread.
The ribs of the brush,
volunteers cut in the sap of their youth,
spit rifle snaps of sound
that ricocheted in the woods,
glowed, heaved, collapsed.

Blackberry runners joined hands
around the encroaching flame at its edge,
taking its heat in their new green,
sapping its kindling power
so that even the stalks of weeds among them,
dry and vincible, smoldered only and smoldered out.
I pushed the charring stubs of sacrificial saplings
toward the heart of the heat,
turning my face away from its blooming potency.
I fed it and built it again with winter's windfalls,
ranging into the cool woods,
my face relieved from the heat,
untangling fallen branches
from the spur-shanked tangle of vines
and dragging them back to their pyre.

Cara came.
To her, it was play of a new kind
(and so it was play, if not new, to me).
Together we fed the fire and talked of what we did,
of McCoy's dog, who barked at me and wagged at her
(she'd known him from puppy up, she said),
of the beetles and tiny bark-hidden bugs we'd save,
if we could, but couldn't, because they were so many
and so hidden (safe they thought, and were right,
except for the unforeseen)
and we must be done before dark.
She left for a while and came again.
Looking across the coals and the little licks of flame,
my back to the terraced hill,
I watched her descend from the house
the opposite wooded slope.
Down she came, gingerly down,
bringing a red paper cup.
Up to my terrace she came,
choosing, choosing her way.
Don't stumble and spill, I prayed,
After so much loving care.
I thought words of comfort in case.
It was Sprite for me in the cup.

The thought was as sweet as the drink, I said,
and she understood, she said.
I took her on my lap by the fire.
We shared the Sprite and talked,
looking into the fluid, translucent depths of the coals,
seeing the long rays of the sun kindle the pines to incandescence,
shielding our eyes from the smoke
when the vagrant breeze would shift.
She said summer was coming
and more beauty even than this.
I said I'd settle for this and such as this:
moments with those I loved best
locked in memory's amber.
She understood, she said.
Some day someone small, someone she loved,
would sit with her, I said, on such a forever day
and later they would remember that
and maybe she would remember this.
Yes, she said, and maybe
we two would still sit like this, too.
That would be nice, I said.
We gathered our things and trudged
up the long opposite ridge to the house.

Later, I looked from the kitchen window
and saw down in the dark,
across where the clearing was,
the last embers.

For a Loved Old Man

And the world was new
and the world was forever
and wish and will be were one.
Now it's time, so nearly time,
to lay him down, and the days,
footprints stippled with wind-drift,
were not as he would
but as they would be. Still,
his they are
and him.
Back they stretch along
the slow warp of ratified fortuity,
softening in windsift,
vanishing far this side
the ground he bestrode in the morning,
and the world was new.

The Girl Behind the Jewelry Counter at Gayfer's

Whether or no there's much to be loved
behind the smile's another thing.
The smile remains. Remains? Wounds
the mind! Self's guardian, Fancy,
rushes in to staunch the harm. The smile
rounds in the eye, limbed and moved
in the smile's image. Promise of *yes*
becomes the flesh of dream, perfect,
willing. The dreaming self itself
stands at the heart of its own myth,
shining, transfixed in the smile's image.

Whether or no there's much to be loved
behind the smile's another thing.
Whether or no . . . Another thing . . .

A Mother Waiting

He died on the beach before Troy, my son.
Homer sang him only as one
of the nameless rabble the names cajoled.
Zeus would protect him, he was told.
Maybe Athena. Perhaps Apollo.
The hope how vain, the promise how hollow.
Our flock he forsook to follow his lord,
and look, just look, what his reward.

And what of me?
Am I not part of that history?
Does my suffering sing through Homer's song?
Have I not languished overlong?
Bards praise but lords. Somehow I must
answer them, answer them from the dust.

Fall

So soon they fall, the leaves.
The thrush has flown, and the faint heart grieves.
Twigs and boughs loom stark
in the cold, grave dark
that comes so soon, so soon.
The sun hangs in the south at pale noon.
In vain, in vain, the sere heart grieves.
Still they fall, float, spin, twist, ride the wind, the leaves.

What's real in them, these shards of dreams? What hope?
Is there no way for us, for me, but down this slope?
Are we, am I, too, doomed to mourn what's past
with no green hope for what's to come at last?
There's this. Fresh, new green will bud and be
for fresh, new eyes to see.

Musing

Is it dried up completely, then?
the little spring that
oozed a tepid wetness tasting
faintly of the fen?

Has it gone dry?
exhausted then from
trying to mount an
everlasting fountain to the sky?

But what is lost?
And must we mark
in mind each dark and marshy
place we've crossed?

Smirk

Lo, a smirk hath come over the land!
The elephant tramples the sharecropper's garden.
Skrik[9] cries out and the bridge leads where?

9 Translates into English as *The Scream*, Edvard Munch's compelling painting.

Woollen wolves in congress assemble.
The soot of enactments stifles the lambs.
Lo, a smirk hath come over the land!

A chasm yawns at the feet of the haven'ts.
Ballot boxes sneer at the needy.
Skrik cries out and the bridge leads where?

Greedheads toy with bigots and clueless.
Gods enrich the cynical saintly.
Lo, a smirk hath come over the land!

Go down, all smug, to thy grave, thou clueless.
Thy children shall wail at the wasting wall.
Skrik cries out and the bridge leads where?

For lo! there's only one Wisconsin.[10]
And woe! even it shall hearken to Texas.[11]
Skrik cries out and the bridge leads where?
Lo, a smirk hath come over the land!

Why

does a poet try to rephrase the world, himself?
Is he another kind of modeler who builds
in miniature the universe, the self,
a model he can hold in his hand, possess,
his own, preserved, scaled down to fit a shelf?

---

[10] Known for its humane legislative and judicial stance concerning the disadvantaged.

[11] Perennial winner of the race to the bottom.

Seekers

In night pre-man was wont to go.
The morning twilight scarce gave pause.
He felt no need to seek Because.
Then hilltop high
In the melon-glow of nearly-know
Loomed How and Why.

And thus began the human race.
In terror of the dawning sky,
Man fled the face of How and Why.
He shunned the morn.
He drew Because a human face,
And God was born?

He brandished God as his Because
And slew upon His cutting edge
The infidels who gave their pledge
To How and Why.
Quite rightly by his new-made laws
The wrong must die.

Then came Because (man thought) full-known,
And temples fell and sore afraid
The fat, God-waving priests were made
To fall and bow.
But from their rubbled altarstone
Rose Why and How.

So man must still grow old and die,
Still stand in awe of sea and storm,
Still hope to find in deiform
The Law of laws.
Is God, alas, the How and Why
Beyond Because?

I Do Not Like Thee, Villanelle

I do not like thee, Doctor Fell.[12]
I do not like this faux relief.
Nor do I like this villanelle.

The reason why I cannot tell.
But I'll be candid and be brief:
I do not like thee, Doctor Fell.

Thy drenches are but draughts from hell.
Their tastes are vile beyond belief.
Nor do I like this villanelle.

I might prefer the passing-bell.
Which thought recalls my plaint-in-chief:
I do not like thee, Doctor Fell.

I loathe thy antiseptic smell.
Thy very voice doth cause me grief.
Nor do I like this villanelle.

This I know, and know full well,
I know it sure as time's a thief:
I do not like thee, Doctor Fell.
Nor do I like this villanelle.

---

[12] Dr. Fell, the archetype, was not a physician, we're told.

Funhouse

I could have used a mirror
that would straighten teeth
broaden shoulders
make eyes soulful

I might have settled for a mirror
that would show me as I am
though I'd not have used it much
liked it much, or me

What I got was a funhouse mirror
and I was the laugh

So I divorced the thing

Red Oak, Tree Deck, and Lake Below

Conceit it is, yes.
Nevertheless:
My grey eyes drink the setting moon
against the coming soon.
Here in the predawn dark
I hear a dog bark,
a rooster crow, a distant truck.
Whether by grace or luck
I sit in the friendly cold
of winter. I'm growing old.

And so,
I pack my thoughts to go:
Memories
of midnight mockingbirds and star-leafed nodding trees,
faces, voices, places,
some leaving only breathless traces,
some graven deep.
There's much to dream before I fall asleep,
much to savour from the cup,
before the sun comes up.

The Reason

Why?
Neither you nor I
can know,
although
we can name whatever reasons,
we can change them with the seasons
of our lives.
Whoever strives

for more certainty than this
must forever miss
the point:
None shall be anointed, none anoint;
no one
shall know the reason; there is none.

Homecoming

Have you heard? He's coming back!
We couldn't do without him after all.
But how he's changed! What, we?
How we see? Nonsense! He's grown.

Did him good, the fall from grace.
Made more than man of him.
A petty man he was at times, too.
Exceeding wroth, indeed! And on the palest provocation.
Like a hard-pressed parent. One expected more.
Never wroth, you say? Or for reasons
better than we know? Siblings' false reports?
But why? Then we were used. And so
was he. To both our hurts.
But see him now! Looks less like us,
though I hesitate to say it. Funny, too:
I like him nonetheless. Different without airs,
I'd say. Now he doesn't force old questions
on us. The ones he answers, though:
Wow! And they're so fresh and ready.
What, we again? It's we, you say, are ready?
I'm damned if I understand you. And damned
if I don't? I might have guessed.
But he won't do the damning, don't you see?
That's the point. He's really changed.
Did him good, I'd say. He never did?
Now look, not that again! He said right here—
Until he left? And then by force of leaving?
I swear, if you don't cut the riddles—
But where's his son? My, as a boy,
how I loved that boy! As I grew up,
he changed. Well, laugh! Go ahead!
I know what you're thinking.
One thing, though: He may have been a fraud,
the boy, but he planned the city well.
Whatever happened to those plans?
They were good plans, even without the promises.
Ah, those promises! How we clutched those promises!
That's what got 'em finally. Both of them.
We don't give our votes for nothing.
No payoff, no vote. No one fools us long.
The old man never promised? The boy
did, though. And he spoke for him.
Because he told us so, that's how!

Well, it doesn't matter now.
Turns out we need the plans, if not the boy.
Need the old man, too.
We had the answers for awhile, but—
Questions are like foothills: Climb one
and right behind it there's another one.
While you catch your breath, you like to feel
you're coming out all right. You can
with a good guide. He is, I guess.
Without him we're off in a dozen directions
and strangers when we meet. With him
I think we'll make it. Here.
And if the promises come true after all—
and they just might, you think?—
Well, that's a little frosting on the cake.
Hey! Hey! Welcome home! Welcome home!

Double Exposure

Two days west at Bosque del Apache
Snow geese lift and settle, lift and settle,
Numbered and restless as driven leaves
lift and settle on the face of winter marshes
Across the fading campus grass in Tuscaloosa.

Aftershave

That bottle's on my shelf
because some girl
whose name and face
I don't remember
said she loved a hint
of Aqua Velva.

Funny
how we mortal planets
tug each other
in and out of orbit
never knowing.

Mestizas y Mestizos

for Rosa Maria Nava

And who is not,
whether within memory or long forgot?
Over every land and island of our Earth,
conquered mothers have given birth
to conquering fathers' progeny,
and this for age on age beyond our kindred's memory,
back and back into the dark
before the garden and the ark.

The conquered's children now and then became
the conquerors, as name
and tongue gave way to name and tongue,
until today, forever older yet forever young,
we find ourselves becoming one again.
Amen . . . Amen . . .

Tell Me

Tomorrow again you had loved life
And the next day and the next.
Oh, now and then,
You had thought this act again.
But then, in the joy of morning,
You had unthought the thought,
Disowned it, wondered at it.
But tell me, tell me,
How unthink the act?

Of Tongue, of Wand, of Hex

Such speech
lies well beyond the reach
of mortals.
Perfection's portals
stand locked against their yearning.
Returning
to the garden there is none.
Nothing here is ever more than just begun.

The blights and frosts repeat, repeat:
no fruits grow sweet;
no harvests but of chaff;
none but the laugh
of ignorance, of superstition;
no telling progress from perdition.

No Faludy, No Havel, No Yeats[13]

And still we are not one.

O, my ornamental masters, Why?
Uncle we not the same Uncle?
Why has our Kindom not come?
Why has not our will, not yours, not mine, not greed's, been done
on earth as it were in the hopeful heart's Eden?

13 Hungarian, Czech, and Irish national poets, respectively.

O, my ornamental masters, When?
Cease to nest and twitter in the gabled eaves of the merchant kings.
Cease to riddle in accustomed codes baubles for each other's dainty hands.
Cease to strip (with little tease) for one another's prurient applause.
You excalibur-tongued, you who'd cut clean, don't leave it to us,
stutter-glottised, hummers-off-key, raisers of welts.
What? Are you servants? Hessians of the tongue?
Slash the networks of blocked and metered prose, mind entangling,
till your tongues' brass edges gleam through the vitriol blue of long disuse.
Shred the threads of inside stories you've spun to mock your kindred many.
Speak, dammit! Right out!

Brave and dreamy Martin, brother in and under the skin,
truest poet, LaMancha's Man,
forsake us not lightly, we thankless deaf and sightless.
But should we, stiff-necked, willful strangers,
reek at last too much of sulphur,
speak then, pray, to the fruit of our wombs, whisper them echoes,
echo them chants at mythic night around the natal fire,
flickering its comfort, fellow-feel, beneath one lithic overhang,
call them, distant issue of nomads, hostile hosts, of armies, empires,
call them in from the lost heart's hunts and the gainless gatherings,
in again to the gendering circle, the nurturing blaze,
as the last dusk falls before the dawn of dawn.

At the Bama: The Scribbler and Others Await the Second Act

Here in seat 59F,
pencil poised over program,
piously praying profundity,
buoyed like kelp in the lift
and surge of intermission's voice,
collective, foamy as surf,
only seals will come to mind,
seals, seals, seals,
thick as papillae on the great,
gray, tumbled tongues of wave-dashed
boulders, charged, ecstatic, locked
in pulsing grids of primal energy.
We come for the crowd.
And the play? Pretense.

Some Poem

Charlotte, matron saint of spinners,
Mother, weave your web for me.
Only you can make of scribblers'
Adumbrations poetry.
In the minds of those who matter,
Magnify my pencil-smatter.

'Bove my work-sty in your nook,
Spin your gauzy magic spell.
Hang it where they'll likely look.
Couplet, sonnet, villanelle:
Help them see the silken purses
In these porky little verses.

Help them feel the metaphor.
Help them see the clever choice
Of novel form and, what is more,
Help them hear a brand new voice.
Spin a web of subtle weaving,
Not to mention mind-deceiving.

Charlotte, mother of all spinners,
Help this scribbler, if you would,
Stand just once among the winners,
Well-connected, if not good.
If you will but grant it to me,
Just a little fame'll do me.

Amen.

Quail

There's shelter in the hedgerows
when the wind begins to bite
and the snow starts stinging beady eyes
the way it does tonight.

It's cozy in last summer's leaves
and safe among the thorns.
The fox won't be out hunting
at least till morning warns.

Crystal fingers span the puddles
that the snowflakes haven't found.
The sloughs are disappearing,
the little ponds, the ground.

The white was cold as carpeting,
but as a roof it's warm,
and little voices chuckle through
brown feathers at the storm.

*

There's no shelter in our houses
from the cold that drives us on,
and our foxes love the blizzard
and they never wait till dawn,

and the thorns that should protect us
tear our hearts and hang us there,
as our whiteness turns to grayness
and our earth grows cold and bare.

Sick and weary of the searching
that has preyed upon our lives,
the cold winds of our winter years
stinging in our eyes,

we know at last we'll never find
a happiness as warm
as to snuggle down and chuckle through
brown feathers at the storm.

Calipers

It's woman's fate to contemplate the stars,
to caliper the Dipper's span.
Challenging face to face the earth,
while life's ecstatic transitory madness grips his soul
is left to man.

Blackhawk

The nth meaning? Yes,
but never in this dress;
never in the shadow of walls
still smoldering; not as morning falls.
Can such lexicology
survive in this geography
thus steepled,
peopled?

Even angels seem otherwise
when thup-thupping blackly down the passes out of blackened skies,
gatling such gospels as they know.
Even so
infernal choirs supernal stanzas sing
when undulating upward on illumined wing.

Sonnet No.3

The gods of odds have willed it otherwise.
But if they would have otherwilled the harm,
I might have been the one to light your eyes
And feel your cheek brush lightly on my arm.
We might have shared the throb of one desire,
And counted wide-eyed cupids our reward.
Then drawing warmth and comfort from our fire,
Have added tenderness unto our hoard.
But someone else is going to live my dream,
To feel your cheek brush lightly on his sleeve,
To kindle in your eyes that cherished gleam.
I may look back just once yet as I leave.
No, there must be one aching backward glance,
For would the gods of odds leave that to chance?

Give me a Going Away Party

as if I were sailing for Australia
and never coming back
but you expected to come see me
some day.

And don't cry
unless you're really sad
that you're not going now
rather than I.

You see,
it's not as bad
this being sent Down Under
as we had thought 'twould be.

Wedges

Glyphs
pock the petrous clay with ifs
and could have beens,
a history of sins
and sacraments
for all intents
as various as our own.
Atone?

We? For them? But how?
Our clay is petrifying even now,
and we,
ourselves astonished by our vanity,
accumulate
our own *too-little* and *too-late.*

Cameos

Santa Barbara at dusk:
from Montecito's shoulders
to green glass, sandal-kissed,
the sweep of vestments

Sandias at sunset:
tawny cat beside the Rio Grande
blushing in her lover's parting glance

Yosemite:
One frame of God's best-selling film, *Eternity*

The sun, the sky, the sea
Eternal links between the race and me

Sleepers in the weeds:
When the ride can be had for lead nickels,
it's a Mensch who gets off
'cause he can't pay with gold.

Metropolis:
Millions who are now the hunted
came here thinking they were hunters.

One boon of you who bless or damn:
It I can't be what I am not,
let me at least like what I am.

The moments I have loved the most:
Dew drops in a spider's fragile web.

Is That All There Is?

It's nice
to have this subtler sense of strokes that will suffice.
But no one here
has been touched by the wand, I fear.
Where's the fire? Where's the ice?

never-mirror lake

slap and rake
slap and rake
ice will come
ice will come
and never break

Proud to Be a Roman?

No . . .
Grateful, though.
There are advantages, you see.
Look at me.
Though not rich, I live well, as many do.
Roman currency spends well the empire through.
But proud? I?
Please tell me why.

Being Roman doesn't add an inch unto my height,
nor does it make me more attractive or more bright.
Nor does it put a penny in the pockets of the poor who shout it loudest,
whom the rulers teach to be the proudest,
to die
for the empire and the rich without really knowing why.

Tally-ho

It's time, it's time that follows me,
that runs me to the ground,
for I'm the fox, the weary fox,
and time, ah time's the hound.

Earth tips her palm toward the sun,
she shows me to the day,
and once again I rise and run;
I fear the breathless bay.

It's time, it's time that follows me,
that runs me to the ground,
for I'm the fox, the weary fox,
and time, ah time's the hound.

He hunts me from the bloody dawn
until the dusk goes black,
against the dread of going on
the dread of turning back.

It's time, it's time that follows me,
that runs me to the ground,
for I'm the fox, the weary fox,
and time, ah time's the hound.

Up hills that make the flanks to heave,
down slopes that bruise the soles,
and oh, the petalled tracks I leave
upon the runnel's shoals.

It's time, it's time that follows me,
that runs me to the ground,
for I'm the fox, the weary fox,
and time, ah time's the hound.

Along the sloughs of wan despair
upon the burrow downs
to stark and sunless moorland where
the hollow sea-moan sounds.

It's time, it's time that follows me,
that runs me to the ground,
for I'm the fox, the weary fox,
and time, ah time's the hound.

Oh, I will run as I can run
and run yet on my knees,
in time begun, by time undone,
dire hound I can't appease.

It's time, it's time that follows me,
that runs me to the ground,
for I'm the fox, the weary fox,
and time, ah time's the hound.

Behind I hear with mortal thrill
the slaver and the pant,
but though my spirit's fleeing still,
my breathless body can't.

It's time, it's time that follows me,
that runs me to the ground,
for I'm the fox, the weary fox,
and time, ah time's the hound.

The wind's dull drum is pendulum,
the bell-cupped breakers toll.
Upon the gust the vixen comes,
the mother of my soul.

It's time, it's time that's followed me,
that's run me to the ground,
I the fox, the foredoomed fox,
and time, ah time the hound.

Night of Nights

We children were nestled all snug and all that.
No one was stirring, not even the cat.
Well, I fibbed there a little. I was awake,
Thanking and thinking of wishes to make.
As I slipped from my bed and knelt for my prayers,
I thought I heard mama and papa downstairs.
Away to the hallway I groped without light,
Crept down to the landing, but stayed out of sight.
And then, at a wave-length I'd not heard before:
A tinkle of bells and chuckles galore!
What then! in a sparkle beyond infrared,
He made himself known, his reindeer, his sled.
Elf is the word. *Right Jolly Old Elf.*
Fly through a keyhole, land on a shelf,
Here for a moment, not thirty days,
Not all over town in a holiday craze,
Not shaking brass bells, not ho-ho-ing in shops,
Not five-nine-two-forty smelling of schnaps.
A fat little Tinker Bell glowing in red,
With a wink of his eye and a nod of his head,
He got right to work. He knew what to do.
And mama and papa were doing it, too!
Each tiny toy that he took from his pack
He put in its place and then he stood back
And pling! there it was! full-size! And, I swear,
It seemed as if papa had just put it there!

Again and again the right jolly old elf
Worked his elf magic. Why, mama herself
Seemed to be putting the doll by the tree.
For I was the only one there who could see
That infrared presence twinkling about
And now and then shouting an infrared shout
As another gift plinged! in its very own place
In the glow of the love from mama's dear face!
It took but a nanosec, though it seemed longer
The tinker bells tinkled stronger and stronger.
I knew he must go now, and he knew it, too.
He had, as you know, a lot still to do.
Up from the bounty he sprang to the shelf
Leaped into his sleigh, that magical elf!
And then he was gone, sleigh, reindeer, and all.
Mama and papa hugged in the hall.
I hurried me back to my bed just before
They came up the stairs and peeked in the door.
Now we children were nestled for real and all that.
Now no one was stirring, not even the cat.
But still at a wave-length elves hear with delight
There was singing and ringing and plinging all night.

Tuscaloosa County's Ridges and Ravines

Sunday morning is the time,
if ever there is a time, to walk
in the brisk essence of luminous autumn,
nude of guilt and the belts and buttons
of care, shuffling, rustling through
the well-spent leaves to knolls
of purer purpose and outlook
such as is afforded by this light.

The bud-taut layers of control
open like hands of generous flowers,
a blossoming not unknown,
even in this penultimate season,
to the patient gatherers, humble, grateful,
meek in the mystery, of this clime.
Still they move, robed and warded
in the mythic mists that flow for ay
in the deep draws of their dimension,
among the hickories of inner sight,
giving as they gather from brown baskets
of earthy weave, following trails,
wispy and imperative, of their being
with step more subtly silent
than ever it was before the tessering
from those untimely woods to these.

Such a time is Sunday morning.
By such steps we tread beyond
the merely necessitous sense,
belts and buttons, even berries
if for the tongue alone, to meanings
leading up from these ravines,
strewn now with crispened leaves
rouged in the earthly shades of this
the second nor penultimate act,
to high divides commanding overlooks,
the late light lengthening
to resurrect the souls of trees,
wherefrom dimension's many
tributary fjords are seen
one as they are or do become
in the infinite amber haze
beyond the reach of reason's eye.

It Was a Dark and Stormy Night

It was a dark and stormy night,
so it's been said.
And well it might
have been.
Who knows how many more
have troubled hearts at times before
and since.
And yet, on moonlit nights
of honeysuckle air and tiny lights
from stars and lightning bugs have harts
been run to ground, have darker arts
played out—in haunted mansions, true,
but even in edens of the few.

What! Can even sunny days begin
To light a dark and stormy night within?

what wonderland this?

soft double delta
fertile moistland
tender tangles
softly briared
Jane-in-the-Pulpit
pinkest petals
worship's grotto

Redstone Arsenal

Who launched this sleek, dynamic shape
without a homing circuit?
What use is such machinery
if no one here can work it?
So what if its trajectory
bids fair to find some mark,
if we can't figure out which one,
can't calculate the arc?
Who programmed such erratic flight?
He'll pay with his dismissal.
For nothing else will do more harm
than a misguided miss'll.

Whose Woods

Whose woods they were you thought you knew,
And where he lived, you knew that, too.
And true, he didn't see you there
Stopped by his woods as twilight grew

And snow descended everywhere,
Hovering in the frosted air.
Your colt shook carols on his bells,
But played his part all unaware

Of dark, deep groves that cast their spells
And to the poet bode farewells.
How could you know what lay before?
The Jiffy Gas, the cheap motels?

For now those woods are his no more,
Nor are they woods. A package store
Looks out upon the frozen lake,
And litter lines the frozen shore.

Ah, surely there's been some mistake?
Dismayed your ghost would see and ache,
But you are spared this cause to weep.
Time's drawn the curtain for your sake.

Still somewhere woods are dark and deep.
But whether you have or haven't kept
The promises you had to keep,
You've gone your miles and now you sleep.

For Amanda Lea[14]

If I were good at poetry,
I'd write a poem for you.
I'd say *I love Amanda Lea*,
And I would mean it, too.

Kiss Me, Kate

Ambivalence
bubbles up
from pools of paradox.
By that act of disloyalty,
you gave me something to live for.

[14] Amanda Lea Boles. Born to Kevin and Cara Boles about noon on July 13, 2005.

Shall hatred be sibling to gratitude?
Thus are the annals of tragedy peopled
and the mythologies of ironic laughter.
Come, Kate, kiss and, if it be so,
so be it, kill and close this history.

A Transient Lectures on Perspective

Singing, you say, for joy
as if his little heart would burst?
Man, let me tell you
how it sounds from here.
It sounds like the public cry
of what should be a very private matter.
Like: *These are mine, these woods, and the modest rosy lady.*
Get your red-feathered tail out now or fight.
It sounds like the red stud
who made my pin-feathers quiver
and who, I suppose, is still
cock o' the woods
till I grow red enough
and loud enough
to put him beyond the great oak.
Right now, in fact,
he sounds like one
who talks a better fight
than I can handle. Oops!
Here he comes again!
G'bye . . . .

The Committee Tours Bryce

As you can see, these folks are only odd in their attire.
Here's a ward of naked ones.
Stop the shivering?
That's our task.
How?
Dress 'em, we think, or thicken their skins.
Here's a wardful dressed in snowsuits.
Not right for Alabama quite?
Quite right!
Ma'am?
But if we do, they're naked underneath.
That ward's already full.
His shirt's too bright?
Please, ma'am, he's on the tour.
No, ma'am, I don't think he's staring at your beads.
Well, maybe I wouldn't wear 'em myself,
but each to his own and the country's free.
As I was saying now . . .

Scrub Oak

When we were young and I almost as tall as they, the pines,
I suffered, for I was the least of all
and stood most in the shade.
When we were new and they as straight as arrows, every one,
I ached to see one shaft not quite so true.
Among the pines, why wasn't I a pine?
Or being not a pine, why was I there?
Every summer added to the hurt that knotted me inside.
My inner shadow grew as gnarled as the one
I cast upon the ground.

And now, they tower above me in the sun, the pines.
Now no shadow taunts me from the ground.
The darker forest shade
has swallowed it forever, yes, and me.
Forever, too, it seems we've lived here side by side.
The sun-hot hate I felt has long since cooled
and died upon the shady forest floor.
These are my friends, if not my brothers, every one.
The wind, the rain, the driving snow, what do I know of these?
My tall, straight-limbed companions shield me from their worst
and give their best to me: caress of breeze,
refreshing drink, and sifting crystal for a winter gown.
The lightning bolts disdain my kneeling, aimless form.
The pines that led them crackling to the clouds
lie split upon the ground.

Don't move me now to slopes not held by them, the pines,
now that the hurt is gone and countless years
lie fallen in the shade.
Don't plant me with the scrubs who still must try,
because there's still a chance to win the prize,
to hunch up highest in the sun and shade the rest.
Why should I hurt again because I cannot be
least gnarled among the gnarled, or the most?
Here at last among the towering all-alikes,
who nod and sigh in nameless sameness, every one,
I know my place, and I know who I am.
Don't rob me now forever of the greatest prize:
the peace that I have found.

For Fum's Birthday, 1983[15]

Words won't do.
A glance, a touch
say I love
and say how much.

With miles between,
the memory
of glance and touch
must do for me.

And may they keep
your heart warm, too,
till glance and touch
say, *I love you.*

Rapunzel

From my niche in the face of the cliff, I can see
a tower as white as the memory
of the princess whose preciousness beckoned me there,
a freckled, pink princess with wind-tousled hair,
and the breezes that fretted her whisper to me
of the fairy-tale days that no longer will be.
For *she's not in her tower*, the breezes sigh.
Oh, she's gone from her tower, good-bye, goodbye.

---

[15] I was visiting at the University of Missouri at Columbia, Missouri, that semester.

A wisp of remembering brings her to me.
We walk and we whisper and touch breathlessly.
There's sun when she smiles and song when she speaks,
the tousled pink princess with dimply cheeks.
And I see the white tower and forget and I smile.
I'll go there and kiss her, it's only a mile.
But she's not in her tower; the smiles die.
Oh, she's gone from her tower, good-bye, good-bye

I held her sweet softness close to me and knew
the fragrance of flowers, the kiss of the dew.
The evenings were precious, the clear morning skies
blessed the bonneted princess with smiling gray eyes.
But her baby-brim bonnet and wind-tousled hair
and the sun and the laughter no longer are there.
For she's not in her tower, I cry, I cry.
Oh, she's gone from her tower, good-bye, good-bye.

My soul longs to drowse in the warmth of its mate.
It goes to the foot of the tower to wait.
But inscrutable forces have darkened the day.
Have mysterious spirits enticed her away?
Please, when will I find her, I ask them, *and where,*
the freckled pink princess with wind-tousled hair.
She's not in her tower, is all they reply.
Oh, she's gone from her tower, good-bye, good-bye.

Visitation will be at . . .

Drifting among you, I sample the eulogies,
breathe the offerings of grief.
I am not here, I had thought to say,
meaning in this somber room.
Confirming our belief, I am risen.
I look down and down on you, the left-behind.

But, I find,
I'm here,
looking down with you upon the left-behind,
thinking of cicadas and cicada shells,
bestowing my *sotto voce* offerings:
Here lies some meager evidence of a past:
unwitting, unwilling link between was
and was to be,
nothing more.
What! Changed the world by some scintilla?
Cause and effect between effect and cause.
I take my leave with each of you,
wafting out upon the heavy, honey-suckled air,
nevertheless still there
in the somber room, lingering,
lingering with the last of you.
Will I attend tomorrow? We shall see.

Occasional Verse

The first leaf fell today, willow
oak,[16] little sternwheel, boatless,
buoyant, pedalling, paddling, down, down
the fluent course, coming to port in the lee
of time time time time time

[16] I think a botanist would describe the shape of a willow-oak leaf as narrow-elliptic, not lobed, toothed, or wavy-edged.

Archilochus colubris (Linnaeus)

Wee bird who hums, you are, whose
wings throb and purr, whose glint-green
self plays on a thread not seen.

Beamed on your full black throat, the
sun's light breaks up band by band,
makes black seem the red of gems.

Analythm

mellow mallow then an ah
lama lama bella noon
donna lawn, donna lawn,
dawning moon then enema
analythm then an ah
mellow mallow then an ah low melanie
mama loan ah then ah then
mama loan ah then
loma linda bella donna lama linda then an ah
lola lola vulva mellow
donde lola mellow mallow
mellow mallow then an ah

Snowing

A fluffy white featherbed covers the meadow,
and the timber is mantled in down.
The chuckling creek lies hushed by the ermine
that's gently subduing the brown.

Fences and roads are hooded or hidden.
Houses and barns wear warm wooly caps
and snuggle, white mufflered, like huge cozy mothers
with man and his creatures asleep in their laps.
The tracks of the animals bred to the stable
won't flaw the new virtue till man says they may.
The scrolls of the wild ones, hunter and hunted,
will be printed tonight, then whispered away.
The feather-spun crystals drift deeper and deeper.
No stain will remain through the night.
The farm isn't ransomed from slush-gray forever,
but just now it belongs to the white.

Nativity Scene

December's on the move. In the folds
of its gusty robes it holds
my forebears' holy season.
Can they lie down together, faith and reason?

Hear it, winter, high in the bony trees?
The furry shiver and puddles freeze.
Where has summer gone, and fall?
Is willed belief belief at all?

Sleet peck-pecks at fallen leaves.
The thrush has flown, and the faint heart grieves.
It finds no comfort in the lexicon.
Where has my inner Christmas gone?

Somewhere here where snow hovers feather by feather?
Somewhere here where white and dusk grow together?
The cedars hold vigil here on the hill.
Can the naked will to believe fulfill?

The hearth waits somewhere down below.
Have I lost all hope in the swirling snow?
Will I find my way home from this whiting dream?
Is it only the gift *of belief can redeem?*

Northwood Lake, Love, and Cellphone

True,
I've always had a thing for you.
I know,
always can't mean more than long ago,
And even *long ago*, may be,
rings a little of hyperbole.

Still,
I'm wont to say I always will.
And when
the nth of always chimes again,
may be we'll find some magic way
to toll the ticking for another day.

You want to know where I am?
Down by the dam
on the cedar bench by the holly hedge
near the water's edge.
The one o'clock sun
warms my back; I'm almost done
resting. This line or two,
and I'll come back to you.

The Fireplace As Theater

Beetle on the burning log,
don't scurry in frenzied circles
while the scorching reaches, reaches!
Run to either end!
Be safe!
You can!

But possible's not possible
when possible's not seen.
You go on toasting there
in circumstances you can't see beyond.

I take intermission in the kitchen,
musing on the meanings of it.

Flat Water[17]

All day the bison
have crossed my mind,

Mephistopheles,
massive and in mass,

rippling the flow,
mudding up the lucid.

Still, above the dust,
the air is clear

all the way back to source,
forward to confluence.

The sky is undistorted blue,
so much as can be,

that old distortion, blue.
It melts along the brim

and in the flow stand out
earth's architectures

---

[17] This poem first appeared in *The Prairie Schooner* many years ago.

only by distance
refracted, and the eye.

I must get closer.
I'll be moving on.

Pick a Prayer

Lord, keep me within the oasis.

Lord, keep the oasis within me
and send me out on the sand.

A Think Tank—Whose?

Do not wake the beast.
Whisper it all gates are pearly,
all gatesmen St. Peter,
all swingings wide provisional,
all turnings away final.

Do not wake the beast.
Play in its ear confections most agreeable.
Nice beast. Beast most justified.
Let it fancy crusts are cake.
Let it dream the blood of honest mirrors.

Do not wake the beast.
Propose it no truth; hum it tales, and softly.
Write it scripts wherein it stars, and nobly,
wherein it righteously bites itself and not
the hand that milks it much and feeds it little.

Do not wake the beast.
Woe! should its nightmares turn to sheep.
If so, zither it green pastures, still waters.
Let it not imagine shearing, bleeding.
Play the shepherd, harp of wolves exotic.

Do not wake the beast.
Beware it walking in its sleep.
Pipe its paws away from gated walls,
its teeth from armored inner sanctums.
Let it trample on its hated tail.

Do not wake the beast.
You who suppose you love the beast, beware,
you who in fantasy ride the beast into battle.
Awakened, the beast loves none, serves none.
It is the beast. It is the beast. It is.

Do not wake the beast.

Of the Master

Worker, know his works and weep.
There is nothing you can do.
Fountains of such reach, such sweep
Always will o'ertopple you.

His artesian sources lay
Deep beneath your cattail marsh,
Plumb it, dipper, as you may.
Truth is truth however harsh.

There is nothing you can do.
Worker, worship where you must.
Give to excellence its due.
Better bowing than unjust.

Truth is truth however stark.
Cheating worth of wonder maims
Cheaters more than those they mark.
Ours the uplift, theirs the names.

Intimations of despair
Seem almost too much for you?
Bear them, worker, persevere.
There is nothing else to do.

Evening Robin As Embodiment of Soul

He alone among the birds sees evening come
and speaks the bittersweet ambivalence we feel.

Apologies

I

When knowinger descendants
of intermediate man
(if such evolve)
pack to leave this smold'ring planet
(if they can)
before it ceases to revolve,
will they take you with them, Shakespeare,
or some extra tubes o' beans?

II

Why go on writing things? he said.
Will they ever make you known?
Or even keep you fed?
I shrugged.
That blind old dog you own,
when did he last bring back a bird?
Face pink, he said,
Once I couldn't drink a fishing hole
fast enough to reach the bank.
He heard and came, old Jim.
He held the pole and held his ground.
I'm here because of him.
Even so, I said.
And now and then,
one of my "things" fishes me out again.

And You, A. MacL.

In the Dark Ages,
nobody thought it was dark.

The sun rose even as today,
wreathed in the lyric of awakenings.

The merchant's wife exclaimed,
How wonderful to live in modern times!

The old men on the wooden bench,
time-soft, remembered the good old days.

We are the Dark Age of a future Now,
falling into shadow as Time's sun
clicks the meridians of the turning wheel.

Southern Pacific Calendar

From the wall I tear a leaf of my life.
It slips through my fingers; I watch it fall in the basket.

So palpable it seems. So palpable it lies there.
Tomorrow's leaf will, too; but then today's?

From the wall is torn a leafless life.
It slips through the fingers. Watch it, watch it fall in the basket.

So palpable it seemed. So palpable it lies there.
Tomorrow's life will, too; but then today's?

Safari on Company Time

Far from my office window to the west
A lead-gray rhino charged along the ridge
Through the dusky-orange afterglow
Earth-bound, at first, he seemed content to quest
But then he dared to stretch his form to bridge
The winds between the sky and hills below

He lost all touch with earth and floated free
And when he did he slipped toward and crossed
The line between the real and the insane
A wild boar, a Spanish bull, and he
Was many other things before he lost
His head and drifted off somewhere to rain

A Passing Breeze

Nod, you tousled tops of summer green.
Pass it on, the breathy code of summering,
those whispers of mysteries astir
among the restless leaves that are, among the restless leaves that were.
The thoughts you entertain, Whither?, Whence?,
let them not disturb the confidence,
the joy, the revelry, the recompense of Now.
Nor let those others trouble you, the Why?, the How?.

It is enough, the honeysuckle breeze.
It is enough, cicadas in the trees.
It is enough, the bark upon the bough.
It is enough, the Here and Now.
It is enough to touch, to taste, to hear, to see.
It is enough to be.

Remembrance in Japanese

for James Dickey

This once-upon-a-cotton-field
brings forth kudzu now.
Its bounty spills across the fence
and tumbles down the grade toward
the rutted old red road.

It sheathes abandoned power-poles
with greenest plush upholstery.
It muslins trees around the field
as if they're haunted easy-chairs,
sofas, tables, chiffonniers.

Somewhere under the smothering green,
an old house grays away,
a husk of clapboard, weathered, warped,
fragile as the crispy, amber shells
of risen cicadas choiring now

in the green heaven of shrouded furniture.
Cicadas? Or echoes of the laughing, crying,
whipping, kissing, cussing, praying
of the last sharecropper family to leave
this place for good? Poor, but proud,

was it hellish heaven or heavenly hell
they left behind, leaving the windows
open, broken, letting them in,
the writhing, coiling vines and other
writhing, coiling things? See,

in the green dark, enthroned upon
the straw and sackcloth mattress
where once passion played and sweat,
the spring-wound, spade-headed,
waiting princess of this verdurous realm.

To you, my once-upon-a-poet:
You ascended, beheld the glory, slept
at the wheel, descended into fame,
and then, and then, with slithering stealth
the kudzu and the copperhead came.

I do not love you

I must not say what now is less than true.
I do not love you now as I did then.
What was is not; *what is* is all there is.

You see, there was so much I could not know.
A drone I was lit on a bloom in blush.
I must not say what now is less than true.

I was so young I did not know that I
but loved you for what seemed to me to be.
I do not love you now as I did then.

For you have changed and now the fall has come.
And now the bloom that blushed has come to fruit.
What was is not; *what is* is all there is.

But sweet the fruit, more sweet than was the bloom.
I taste it soul to soul and it is good.
I must not say what now is less than true.

I do not love you now as then I did.
I did not love you then as now I do.
What was is not; *what is* is all I need.
I have not said what now is less than true.

Rose and Bee in Landscape

The rose had no unlovely part
So fair and beautiful to see
Surely nectar from its heart
Would warm and fill the hopeful bee

Gentle rains in loving measure
Had caressed the pretty flower
The sun had lavished all its treasure
On its favorite, hour by hour

Surely now a wandering bee
Could hope for rest and sweetness there
A rose so blessed and fair to see
Must have treasures it would share

Vainly, though, he tried to cling
To plastic petals, bright and smart
Held together, ring on ring
By a sponge, the rose's heart

The nectar that it had for sale
Was raindrops hoarded one by one
That tasted like the sponge and stale
From standing too long in the sun.

He's gone. And though the hill is bare
The lonely rose looks lovely still
Though now no gentle rains fall there
And though the sunless sky is chill

Regret

If I cry
when you die,
it won't be because you had to go,
or because of the reminder
that I will have to go.
No, I'm reconciled to that.
It will be because of things
we could have talked about,
but didn't;
because of things
we could have done as one,
but didn't;
because of love
I could have shown
while you could see,
but didn't.

Stumbling Along

Looking forward to mirages
and backward at shadows
I stepped on today

Those we love become for us
the meaning of beauty. Thus,
don't ask me, *Am I or no?*
The question lost its meaning long ago.
Only a stranger, if asked, might know.

While My Child Sleeps[18]

Cara, cara,
what can I, all-knowing,
-doing, promise you?
The crab, the vise, the wheel,
the weight of seasons.
And yet,
between the echo in
(black velvet)
and the echo out,
there's hope
forever hope
beyond hope,
the game trotzdem,

[18] My daughter was three years old when I wrote this. She is now a physician and mother.

helping those in need,
and inner peace.
There's How and Why
unanswered: the quest
that opens on a dream
or dreams on into velvet once again.
What more could I,
All-Knowing,—Doing,
pledge my princess?

The Pervasive Evasive Electrostructure

psychic wheel, underpowered	:	desperate equation:
in essential frame	:	imbalance in mortal perpetuity
nodding allusively	:	rolling to tipping point
on a gilt propriety	:	of THE solution:
		potential and kinetic,
		accelerating out-of-phase harmonics
		around unity
		resolving implosively to zero

Return of the Native 2

I go back to my native plain
for funerals, to share the pain
of loss, the awe of death,
with my remnant tribe who there enraptured still draw breath.
Hear how they comfort one another with the words of hope
we learned together as truth, not trope.
I acquiesce.
Why should I blight, when I can bless?

And yet,
to acquiesce, to silently affirm this language does abet
their urge to claim
omniscience, omnipresence, for the name,
the very name, the om! they chant against the gargoyle's leer,
to will that all shall bend the knee, shall love, shall fear
this very name and not another.
One who doesn't is no brother,
and, soon or late,
the ties that bound uncoil, recoil, and strike with hate.

Renascence

. . . and seal this chamber off?
Encrypt its spirits of the dead?
Why not instead
open windows in it; clear the cough
of musty memories from the vault?
Size and tint the dank stone walls and gloomy cope.
Make of its space a studio of hope.
Exorcise those ghosts, abuse and fault.

But ward it now before the light's let in,
before the Cheshire grin
of circumstance has dimmed away,
before the minty breeze has cleared the fragrance of decay,
and while the gloom
with bony finger beckons from the room.

Me

is a shadow
we cast upon our lives:
roiling clouds,
thunder,
lightning,
wind,
dust,
and no rain.

"New Voice"

Please! Trite me no more trites!
By rights,
the next to say or write "new voice"
boils in ink while choirs of linguaphiles rejoice.
No more cliches!
The eyes glaze,
the mind takes leave,
longs, longed, has longed for some reprieve.

In short,
reviewers, critics, others who survey the sport,
do as said, not done,
by those who run
the race, who do the verse.
Do better! Or at worst, no worse.

I rode aloft

and loved the craft
that took the waves
ah! how it took the waves
and lo, a trough
ay, now and then
but wallow, nay!
the crests, the crests,
we saw them, I,
challenge and vista, both
and pride
ah! the craft, the waves
the whelming waves
the pride

and now
I ride
inside
the crests, the crests
they're there
somewhere
above the jade deep wall
ah! shooshing white
calling
pulling
hauling
me aloft
Aloft! Aloft!
or drown!
the voices sing

or yet grow gill
and web
or wing?

Fourth Dimensional Harmony

This tie on this shirt recalls the grays that pleased me,
painted on the plywood head of the hobby horse
made by my father for me that pleased me.
What's that twinge? Recall? Remorse?

Why She Did It

Anguish grew
like a black balloon
became the world
to bursting

Untitled Morning

Hop by hop, the juncos anticipate the lawn,
I thought from my ledge at the window.
The loomy zoysia reeked in the rain like wet wool.
That cardinal dabbed thus on the nap,
I thought, *contradicts the calm.*
The master, unseen, granted my judgment,
brushed the cardinal out. Instead,
a mockingbird appeared,
grayer than calm, or the mist.
The tick of the rain, its tock from the eaves
tolls the heart's pendulum, I thought,
and the cold crept. *Please, the cardinal.*

The master's hand tempered my judgment with mercy,
sprinkled the lawn with finches. *Thanks*
for the speech of the thrasher, I thought,
That broguey bird sings welcome counterpoint
to the rain's relentless logic. And then,
what cheer there was in thoughts of loss
trilled memory's obbligato. *The juncos*,
I said with a start, *are gone. How*
did I miss their parting flash of white?
Brown as old wool and wet, the grass,
and the cold mist crept.

One Puff

The cards fall in upon us: aces, jokers, deuces, treys.
The father builds, the son enjoys, the grandson pays.
How could they not have known:
When evil profits ill, good must atone,
Yes, even down to generation seven
And beyond. Heaven
Here on earth or heaven hereafter
Goes up in smoke and drifts away to futile laughter.

How otherwise it might been.
Those whose calculating and successful sin
Usurped the people's voice
Might have made the general good their choice,
Not their narrow avarice.
May they never rest in peace.

Amused

If owning lies in will alone,
no poem's my own.
Through the hum
of hives, words come.
Or not.
Either yes, or nothing gets begot.
Once again, the sun, through dawning blue,
rises to nothing new.

And yet, my own tongue dumb,
when I, amused, hear something catchy come,
I play
amanuensis for the day
all unaggrieved, instead,
giving quiet thanks to be so visited.

Untitled Binge

i

This Bud's for me:
O, most benevolent eye,
placental guardian,
who smiled your jaundiced light upon me in the yolk,
who crossed with me the threshold of the universe,
winking, winking most jestfully,
would you had looked daggers, greatest gift.

ii

This Guinness, too:
Most merciful mirror,
could you but always look away,
I'd sing your praises,
shout you to the pantheon.
Then could I laugh
with my optic angel at her joke.

iii

And this merlot:
I repent,
I have repented me,
this troika, this sunderer
of reason, rhyme, and rhythm.
This, too, my jaundiced angel,
my reflecting pool?
Surcease!

iv

A toast:
A curse upon your cosmic rays
and your unsequenced DNA,
upon your gargoyle mirror
and your yellow light.
Allow me this,
or I must curse you
face to faceless face.

To One Alone

Are you lovely? Yes,
but that's been said before.
Are you gifted, charming? Yes,
but if I say no more
than that, I shouldn't speak
at all. You are my home.
I am content, no longer seek.
The faithful beating of my metronome
says and again, again: *You're my home.*
You're my home. You're my home.

Winter Solstice

Snow falls.
An aging man in overalls
walks beside the Osage orange hedge
grown up through the fence along the edge
of an abandoned pasture overgrown
with scrubby cedar trees. He's alone,
but for the ghosts of long ago,
leaving feathery footprints around his in the snow.

And look!
His footprints close behind him, chapters in a book.
His specter disappears
beyond the veils of falling snow, of years.
With him these ghosts will die,
leaving the snow alone beneath a sullen sky.

To Whom Most Loved

Love is not soup ladled into cupped hearts.
I love you with all my love,
and you with all my love, and you,
and it is the same love, for each, for all,
today the same as yesterday,
tomorrow still the same,
not being less by loving,
not growing cool by loving,
but filling as it fills,
warming as it warms.

Love is our faces' images
embraced in facing mirrors
reflecting, echoing forever.

To Hear Oneself Talk

Today,
could I but go away,
I would.
For good.
To where?
I wouldn't even care.
Would you?
Perhaps I'd stay if you asked me to.

Outsider

There can be no question, there can be no doubt:
the posturing poet has been left out.

He stands on the sideline looking wise;
if he can't take part, he'll criticize.

He stands on the outside looking sad.
Now isn't that too goddamn bad?

Kyrie

The Lord lift his countenance upon me
And give me peace.
For though I have walked in the Valley of the Sun,
I have walked in shadows.
And though I had strode with seven-league strides,
I doubted I knew the way
And so have trod in place.

My God, my God,
Why have I forsaken You?
And had I not, where had I been today?
But woe, by seeking You
I only seek a place on higher ground,
Then woe, I am not seeking You,
And You will not be found.

Father, Father,
Who are You but reflection of me?
And if this be true,
Then how am I to see the way
I doubt I know? And lo,
By seeking You will I find only me?
And then, if so, shall I expect
The me I seek or the me I flee?

God be with me and with my spirit.
Though my spirit has descended into darkness
And gropes in labyrinths uncharted,
Yes, by Him who knows not fear and doubt,
Uncharted, unsounded, unsoughtout,
Be with me now and in the hour
When all is lost to me and I
project Him on a vacant sky.

Lord, have mercy, Christ have mercy.
Lave the fire in my brain.
Burn it clean and cool or quench it utterly.
Sear me oh sear me not
On a pyre of my own volatile images.
Let there be cool and a breath of promise,
And may the *Kyrie, Kyrie,* be of a falcon flying,
Not of the spirit dying forth above the fire.

The Lord bless me and keep me.
Keep me from the mirror waters
of the mind's merciless eye.
Keep me, Keep me from the blessings of abundance.
Free me from the hunger for hunger
For honest hunger's sake.
Let me know what I seek
and bless me, bless me with it
Or with knowing it is not.

So be it. So be it.
So be it, if You will.

Tea Time

But it has to have a meaning.
I mean, we can't be here for nothing.
Why? Because.
Was all of this just made without a plan?
All creation squandered aimlessly?
Surely not, and well,
there just has to be.

Who is that ugly little man?
Leering at us through the window there.
So smug. He ruins everything.
Can't you make him go away?
Well then, if he won't go,
let's pull the meaning down.
Oh damn, I mean the shade.

There.
As I was saying now,
it has to have a meaning, don't you think?

By the Warrior River at Flood

There is no smell of death.
The smell of death is the breath of feasters,
Alive, vibrant, as deserving as we.
Death is no where and no thing.
It rates less than five lines.

A brave stance.
And yet, in the cold dawn,
still too weak with sleep to take it on,
see how on the knees and to what tune you dance.

The Civil War Dead Pass in Review

we poured our precious powder and we tamped unwieldy wadding
and we fed 'em pretty pewter that was better off as plates
we killed our friends 'n' brothers and we killed some goddamn others
and we kept on stormin' ridges till we reached the fiery gates
we fought through sheets of fire and through bodies pilin' higher
and the blood that wasn't soakin' blue was surely soakin' gray
now the muskets and the mortars and the sabers and the orders
and the fightin' and the dyin' all are over for the day
and we march by gaunt 'n' yawnin' from these many years o' sleepin'
and our uniforms are musty and you can't tell blue from gray
and our uniforms are musty and you can't tell blue from gray

Shrub

Guess
who's party to this knuckle-headedness?!
Again!
Since when
can make-believe stand in for reason?
Is asking *Why?* the same as treason?
Is asking *How?* unpatriotic?
Is faith in feeling not quixotic?

Ah, Shrub!
herein lies the rub.
By the time we're quit of you,
there may be nothing we can do
at all
to stem America's decline and fall.

Southern Snowfall

Sadder but wiser
Earth robes herself again
in innocence of snow.

Thus the casual solipsist speaks,
but oh, could he but wear
that robe again and know

at each sad putting off
there'd be another putting on,
a new embrace of promise.

No, no, this token snow,
so quickly evanesced,
so soon to yield to merest

glimpse of light, is not
the symbol of the soul's need.

.

Sad solipsist, cold and naked
when delusion fails, what new
pretense remains to be put on?

Do not despair. Our senses
still protect us from the true
we but suspect. To think

is not to know. Don't dwell
upon that sad estate in which
uncertainty is solace. Speak

your will, your happy order.
See the world's old atomies
array themselves again

by the light of your very eye.
Thus seen, illusion was the real
our mothers moved among,

surviving, flourishing. Shall we,
the heirs of major mind, unleash
that mind upon ourselves, wake us

from the senses' saving dream
that we, however poignantly awake,
may freeze among the tatters

of a world, for all its doubtful
substance, real enough to hand us
down? Can mind go on alone?

If not, what compromise
must still be bargained for
and bought within the secret rooms

of this, this one so strangely two?

.

.

Keep on. Step for step the trek
that brought us here surviving,
still must lead us on. Pray

we not arrive. Horizon's reach,
however wished, is journey's end.

.

Our hopeful tracks are marked
in memory by the spanning snow.

.

The snow is melting, melting.

.

.